A BEGINNER'S GUIDE TO RADIO
Fourth Edition

F. J. CAMM

This photograph of F.J. Camm surrounded by a class of students, apparently giving a lecture about radio, was posed for his book on the subject. It was a throw-back to the days when F.J. taught drawing and mathematics.

See Practical Wireless, August 1955, page 471

Preface

F.J. Camm 1895-1959 of Windsor

It has been difficult to put all his activities into a logical order because of their variety. He was a prolific author, and editor of seven *Practical* journals. He was a prodigious reader, keen to keep abreast of innovative technology. His readers consulted him, and made use of the free advice facilities of the journals. He became affectionately known as "F.J."

Frederick James Camm was born on 6th October 1895, the second child in a family of 12. His eldest brother was Sydney Camm, who designed the famous Hurricane fighter aircraft of the last war. They lived in a "two up and two down" terrace house, 10 Alma Road, Windsor.

When eight years old, he became a Foundation Scholar at the Royal Free School, where he excelled at mathematics, technical drawing and religious knowledge – for which he won the Champagne Trust prize bible in 1910.

In 1911 Sydney and F.J. started the famous Windsor Model Aeroplane Club which built and flew models, and progressed to a series of man-carrying gliders, the third of which they planned to fit with an engine and fly around the Round Tower of Windsor Castle, a project foiled by the outbreak of war in 1914.

F.J. left school in 1910 and was apprenticed for seven years to Brown Brothers of Windsor, prestigious coach builders. With a work force of about 60 men, and a superior reputation and clientele, F.J. gained valuable experience. They dealt with the Lord Mayor's coach.

His father Frederick William was a journeyman carpenter, with a reputation as a high class workman. His mother was one of the Smith family who provided fairground rides at Egham and Eton – the Camm boys used to be given pockets of pennies by their cousins to spend at the fairs.

His grandparents had been named "CAM" until prize certificates awarded by the Royal Association spelled their name as "CAMM" and his grandfather said "What was good enough for the Queen was good enough for him".

In 1918 F.J. obtained work in London, and was soon employed as Technical Editor on aviation and science publications for Benn Brothers, and other publishers. He became a keen massed start road cycle racing enthusiast. He built models – and, with a younger brother George, built the *Cambro* cycle car in 1919 – used to visit Sydney and his wife at Byfleet.

Benn Brothers published his first book *The Design of Model Aeroplanes* in 1919. This soon needed a second edition. He married Dorothy May Field, and set up home in Grove Road, Windsor. Then came work with Pitmans, from which he was encouraged to follow his friend Molloy to George Newnes to produce the *Hobbies* journal and annuals. These included his supplement on *Practical Wireless*, which became so popular that in 1932 it developed into the first of the *Practical* journals F.J. was to edit for Newnes. *Practical Mechanics*, and five other *Practical* journals followed, plus more than 117 technical books for which he was the author or editor. His instruction manuals, text books and encyclopaedias were eagerly read, and are still collected with pleasurable nostalgia by those who recall one or another of his variety of technical specialities. Model aeroplanes, radio, television, and radar technician, cyclist, motorist and small car designer, mechanic, watchmaker and repairer, journalist and lecturer, he was jack and master of several trades and crafts at George Newnes Tower House Strand offices. Fond of the

F. J. Camm
The Practical Man, 1895-1959
An Outline of his Life and Works

Gordon G. Cullingham

First published in 1996 by the author
Gordon G. Cullingham
Windsor

Copyright
Every effort has been made to obtain copyright clearance, subject to the new E.U. Directive. The CAMM family authorised the writer to use their material and otherwise copyrights are reserved by the writer and use is subject to acknowledgement.

ISBN 0 9528448 0 X

This publication is number

424

of a Limited Edition

Designed and printed by
Thameslink Ltd
Windsor 01753 620540

classics, he would meet friends at the Ostrich Inn at Colnbrook. He was taken ill at work where he was to be found at weekends after the death of his wife and only son, and died in February 1959.

I am grateful to all those who have shared their enthusiasm and knowledge of F.J. Camm and his works without which this biography could not have been compiled. I did not have the advantage of knowing F.J. during his lifetime, and I have depended upon the availability of published records, and the personal reminiscences of those who have first-hand knowledge.

The Windsor Local History Publications Group with the aid of British Aerospace and the Royal Borough arranged for a memorial plaque to be put on 10 Alma Road, Windsor where Sydney Camm was born on 5th August 1893.

The Mayor of the Royal Borough of Windsor & Maidenhead, Cllr. Richard Shaw, unveiled the plaque on 12th March 1986, this being the 20th anniversary of Sir Sydney Camm's death.

F.J.'s works are his memorial, and the Royal Windsor "F.J. Camm" collection. I offer my apologies for errors and omissions.

Gordon G. Cullingham
Windsor, SL4 3HA
1996

Acknowledgements

I am grateful for valuable help given by members of the Camm family and organisations including Aeromodeller, The Royal Albert Institute Trust, The Royal Borough of Windsor and Maidenhead, Friends of the Windsor and Maidenhead Royal Borough Collection, Windsor Local History Publications Group, The National Motor Museum Trust, The Princess Margaret Rose Royal Free School Windsor, S.M.E.E. Model Engineering News, SAM 35 SPEAKS and all the "F.J. Camm" enthusiasts who kindly supplied valuable details including , Mr and Mrs R. Ham, Alex Imrie, Derk Rouwhorst, Les Rix together with *Practical Wireless, Practical Mechanics, Practical Motoring, Practical Householder* and the Amberley Museum, also Thameslink for relieving me of the problems of publishing.

Contents

Preface	iv
Acknowledgements	v
List of Illustrations	viii
Early Aviation	1
The Wright Brothers, Patrick Y. Alexander, and the Bee Keeper of Ohio	1
Early Aeronautics	2
School days and early model aeroplanes	4
How did it all start in Windsor?	4
The Wright Brothers aviation news comes to Windsor	5
The Wokingham Whale	7
The Taplow Gyropter	8
The Benton Air-Car	8
The Camms and Aviation	9
The First Flights to Windsor in 1911	10
The Windsor Model Aeroplane Club is formed in 1911	12
Extract from 'Flight' dated September 3rd, 1915. 'The Loading etc., of Models'	13
Windsor Aero Club (from the Windsor Express, 15th November 1913)	17
The Windsor Model Aeroplane Club	20
Two Camm marriages, and F.J. becomes Editor for Everyday Science	21
The Camms and the 1914-18 Great War years, and F.J. starts work as a Technical Writer	22
The "Cambro" Cycle Car, of 1919	27
F.J. Camm and The Design of Model Aeroplanes with Foreword by Frederick Handley Page	29
Flying the Atlantic project	30
F.J. Camm's The Design of Model Aeroplanes (1919)	31
How did the Camm pilots learn to fly the W.M.A.C. gliders?	32
F.P. Raynham and the first King's Cup Air Race	32
F.J. The Glider Pilot	33
Model Flying Machines designed by F.J.	34
F.J. Camm and the Model Engineer exhibition of 1935	41
F.J. Camm the Cyclist and the "Werner" model	42
The Propeller competition of 1922	43
F.J. and Draughtsmanship and Handbooks	48
F.J.'s Publishers	48
F.J. becomes an Editor	51
Wireless Telegraphy	51
Wireless Telegraphy Tuition	52
The Home Electrician	53
Practical Wireless	56
Practical Television and F.J. Camm	56
F.J. Camm and Radar	64
F.J.'s Miscellaneous Publications	64
F.J.'s Coterie	66
F.J.'s Pseudonyms (and obsessions)	66
F.J.'s Patents	67
F.J. The "Eminent Wartime Journalist"	68
F.J. Camm and "Practical Mechanics'" Silver Jubilee	70
Our Silver Jubilee and the Three Wheel £20 Car	71
The Four Wheeled Midget Car of May 1937	73
F.J.'s other Practical Journals	80
Practical Engineering	82
F.J.'s "P.M. Blueprint" Service	83
Practical Motorist	83
Practical Home Money Maker	84
The Practical Series	85
F.J. goes to Law	85
Legal Notes	85
The Greenly Episode	88
F.J. Relaxes	88
The Ostrich Inn, Colnbrook	89
The Camms and the V.E. Day Celebrations, May 1945	91
F.J. The Model Maker	92
Practical Wireless celebrates 60 years of publication, October 1992	94
F.J. The Editor – A Summary	94
Periodicals associated with F.J. Camm	95
References	95
Libraries and Museums	95
Institutions with F.J. material in Library	95
F.J.'s editorships	96
Following in F.J.'s Footsteps and The Obituaries	96
Appendix	100

List of Illustrations

F.J. Camm 1895-1959 of Windsor	Frontispiece
F.J. Camm surrounded by a class of students	iii
The artists' idea of flight in 1959 – '50 Years Hence'	3
From an Aero Manual book dated 1909 – All about Mechanical Flight	3
The Camm family home, Windsor	4
Patrick Y. Alexander (1867-1943)	6
The Wokingham Whale on a horse drawn cart in 1910. St Leonards Road, Windsor	7
The Wokingham Whale outside the entrance to the cemetery, St Leonards Road, Windsor	8
T.O.M. Sopwith on the East Lawn at Windsor Castle, 1st February 1911.	11
Driver's Arrival in Windsor Great Park	11
The penny magazine 'Flight'	12
George Camm and the Cowley Aero Engine	15
The first club card	16
Windsor Aero Club members	17
The W.M.A. & G. Club glider	18
"The Glider in the Air"	18
The W.M.A. & G. Club members, 1912	19
The W.M.A. Club second glider, Windsor Home Park, 1913	19
Elevations and plan of W.M.A.C. Glider, 1922	20
F.J.'s Marriage Certificate 1919	21
F.J.'s Model Airship plan and Model Airship "In Flight"	23
The Camm five cylinder compressed air model engine	23
A Model Long Distance Monoplane type 1-1-P2, 1918	24
The 'Home Mechanic' Series and Model Aeroplanes and Airships	24
A Model Monoplane type 1-1-P2, 1918	26
The 'Cambro' Cycle Car, front and rear	27
The 'Cambro' Cycle Car literature cover	28
A Tractor Monoplane	31
A Tractor Biplane	32
A Single Screw Monoplane	34
A Twin Screw Monoplane	38
A Petrol-driven Model Monoplane	41
Prize winning model of the 1897 Werner.	42
Competition Propellers	45
Static Thrust Measurement Apparatus	47
Authors Foreword: Hobbies New Annual.	48
Authors Foreword: The Model Aircraft Book.	49
Practical Wireless Vol. 1 Cover	54
"On Your Wavelength" by Thermion	55
Practical Wireless, November 7th, 1932 – The "Argus 3"	57
Practical Wireless, The Editor's Brief History	58
Practical Wireless, 21st Birthday Number Editorial	61
Practical Wireless, 'My 21 years as an Editor, 1932-1953'	62
Issue No. 1. Practical Television	63
A new or Improved Collapsible Pont or Pontoon	67
Phosphoric Lighter	68
Pneumatic Tyre Inflator	68
Worlds Press News, May 28th 1942	69
A typical Practical Mechanics jacket	70
Cut-away View of the £20 3-Wheeled Car	71
'Our Silver Jubilee' – article	72
Building our £20 Car	74-77
The £20 3-Wheeled Car of 1936	78
The £20 4-Wheeled Midget Car of 1936	79
Practical Householder, advert	80
Practical Mechanics, advert	80
Practical Mechanics, Blueprint Service	83
Practical Home Money Maker	84
Infringements resulting in advertisements of regret, damages and costs	86
The Bassett-Lowke 50th Anniversary Dinner in 1949	87
F.J. and Freddie's Christmas card, 1957	88
F.J. Camm, Mrs Dorothy May (Field) Camm & Little Fred in bucket and spade days	89
The Ostrich Inn, Colnbrook, Murder Bed	90
V.E. 1945 Day, Saturday 19th May 1945	91
The section of a four cylinder engine built	93
The Burrell type traction engine, introduced by Bassett-Lowke Ltd.	93
Practical Motorist Obituary	97

Early Aviation

The Wright Brothers, Patrick Y. Alexander, and the Bee Keeper of Ohio

This is based upon conjecture, and a little circumstantial evidence. In December 1905 Patrick Y. Alexander of Bath and Windsor received a letter dated 17th November 1905 from his friends the Wright Brothers about their flights. They had written him before – on one occasion with an invitation to attend their first circular flight, but the letter was delayed, and he went to Blue Hills near Boston instead.

P.Y.A. read the letter to the (Royal) Aeronautical Society on 15th December 1905 and shortly afterwards gave a talk on aviation to the United Services College, Alma Road, Windsor near where the Camms lived. It seems reasonable to assume that the latest news from the Wrights would be mentioned to the boys.

At that time, Sydney was 12 years old, and F.J. was 10. The only known press report of the first powered circular flight had been the scoop of a lifetime of Amos Ives Root of Medina, Ohio – a bee keeper – in his magazine *Gleanings in Bee Culture*. Other publications turned the story down as an "outlandish fairy tale".

The Wrights' earlier invitation to P.Y. Alexander had been to come to Huffman Prairie, Dayton, Ohio to "look over their latest Wright Flier". This had flown a half circle on 15th September 1904. Their first Flier had flown four times on 17th December 1903, but only in a straight line.

Then came the famous flight on 20th September 1904. The press had been invited to attend other proposed flights, but a series of minor troubles prevented any take off, and the pressmen left, never to return.

It is said that three people witnessed the historic flight by Wilbur, one a neighbour of the Wrights, Mr Taylor, also Orville Wright, and Amos Ives Root.

The following is extracted from the contemporary account written by Amos, who headed his article ***"What hath God wrought?"***

> *God in his great mercy has permitted me to be, at least somewhat, instrumental in ushering in and introducing to the great wide world an invention that may outrank electric cars, the automobiles, and all other methods of travel, and one which may fairly take a place beside the telephone and wireless telegraphy ... It was my privilege, on the 20th day of September, 1904, to see the first successful trip of an airship, without a balloon to sustain it, that the world has ever made, that is, to turn the corners and come back to the starting-point ... When it first turned that circle, and came near the starting-point, I was right in front of it; and I said then, and I believe still, it was one of the grandest sights, if not the grandest sight, of my life. Imagine a locomotive that has left its track and is climbing up in the air right towards you – a locomotive without any wheels, we will say, but with white wings instead. Well, now, imagine this white locomotive, with wings that spread 20 feet each way, coming right towards you with a tremendous flap of its propellers, and you will have something like what I saw. The younger brother bade me move to one side for fear it might come down suddenly; but I tell you friends, the sensation that one feels in such a crisis is something hard to describe ... When Columbus discovered America he did not know what the outcome would be, and no one at that time knew. In a like manner these two brothers have probably not even a faint glimpse of what their discovery is going to bring to the children of men. No one living can give a guess of what is coming along this line ... Possibly we may be able to fly **over** the north pole, even if we should **not** succeed in tacking the 'stars and stripes' to its uppermost end."*

Subsequently there were other claimants to have "Flown First", but this impeccable eye witness of the flight in September 1904, long before any serious European claim to have flown, was from someone who had committed the whole experience to paper and published it in his journal – a journal that is still published by one of his descendants in Medina, Ohio where it started. The article is dated 1st January 1905 and extends over four double-column pages of the journal. It is also the first eye witness account of a powered flight in the history of aviation.

Thus, P.Y. Alexander had the Wrights' letters, he gave talks about aviation to the boys in Alma Road, Windsor. Sydney and F.J. were in touch with Eton College boys from time to time, and, about model aeroplanes – (although there is no record) – similarly with the United Services College boys. Surely news of Amos Root's vivid article reached the Camms?

In 1909, imagination was confined to the artists' ideas of "50 years hence", as in the illustration below published in *The Motor*.

The illustration and the description below is taken from an *Aero Manual* book dated 1909 *All about Mechanical Flight*. Compiled by the staff of *The Motor*, with 150 illustrations it was published just before Bleriot's successful flight across the English Channel.

Early Aeronautics

By 1914 catalogues of goods that came under the title *Home Scientist* were offered by Gamages of Holborn and Benetfinks of Cheapside. The model railways, yachts and kites of Victorian and Edwardian days were augmented by model aeroplanes, also dynamos and electric motors and batteries.

Aeronautics, a weekly journal devoted to the technique and industry of aeronautics claimed to have been founded in 1907, was priced 6d (2½p) weekly.

The journal for the growing electrical industry was "*The Electrician* established 1861" and this weekly was also priced 6d.

Many firms offered materials for constructing model aeroplanes, including the Warmley Aeroplane Company of Bristol, the BIRMAC Aeroplane company of Tottenham, A.E. Jones of New Oxford Street, London, with many others including Drake Engineering Syndicate (Chingford), Taplin Bros, mechanical engineers of Hornsey Road, Roberts Engineering Co (R.E.C.O.) of Old Street, City and Aero Models Ltd of West Byfleet.

In 1909 an *Aero Manual* had been compiled by *The Motor*, which claimed a circulation of 43,000 copies weekly and that "the trend of events in mechanical flight and aeronautics, is thoroughly dealt with and illustrated in *The Motor*".

This publication had a frontispiece "50 years hence" (reproduced elsewhere) and a preface by Professor Chatley BSc, A.M.I.C.E., Imperial Engineering College, North China entitled "Aeroplane, Design and Construction".

Regulations for pilots were defined as:

If, beneath you, planes appear,
It is your duty to Keep Clear
To act as judgement says is proper,
To port or starboard – rise, or drop her!

Apparently it was expected that navigation in the air would be governed by the same rules as control the navigation of ships at sea.

The *Aero Manual* including the Gliding Experiments of the Wright Brothers, with a caricature of Wilbur Wright "The Man and the Machine". In 1906, three years after the Wrights had achieved powered flight, this was not generally believed especially in France, but the possibility incited everyone to increased

The artists' idea of flight in 1959 – '50 Years Hence'

OUR FRONTISPIECE.

The scene, as observed from the pilot's seat of an aeroplane, 50 years hence, will show great departures from present-day methods of locomotion. The difficulty of the aeronaut in ascertaining his whereabouts has been overcome by the artist. To meet the many difficulties the highways have been considerably widened, the broad road for motor traffic being bordered on either side by great green swards, which serve as landing places for flying machines. Over these great trackways flying machines may travel, and, to facilitate night travelling, each trackway is bordered with a broad band of white chalk so that the searchlights of the flying machines may pick out the road boundaries. Each road is given a distinguishing symbol, the great national roads being lettered N R and numbered. Thus the aeroplane in the picture is travelling over N R—71, the great north road between London and York, whilst branching to the left is C R—3, the county road to Peterborough. The names and the signs are all laid in white chalk set into the green grass, and the name of each place is similarly shown as clearly as possible. The artist has assumed that navigation in the air will be governed by the same rules that control the navigation of ships at sea. A new regulation is needed only for the variation of altitude. It can be defined by a parody on the verse that refers to ships crossing:

> If, beneath you, planes appear,
> It is your duty to keep clear;
> To act as judgment says is proper,
> To port or starboard—rise, or drop her!

Flying clubs can be seen in the picture at a couple of points, and the Aero Hotel at Norman Cross has made ample provision in the way of landing space and machine storage.

From an Aero Manual book dated 1909 – All about Mechanical Flight

effort to get a mechanically-driven machine to rise from the ground and maintain itself in the air. Gliders were flown by power obtained by towing the glider with a car. Less wealthy airmen used ropes pulled by horses or youths, or from a falling weight. Some favoured airships. In July 1903 the first successful Zeppelin had flown over Lake Constance, viewed by Patrick Y. Alexander.

The *Aero Manual* devoted six pages to "How to construct a glider. Instructions for learning to glide". Both Sydney and F.J. published similar details in 1919. A.V. Roe and his Avroplane – with its engine that Sydney Camm later bought – this machine was regarded as "underpowered" in 1909 – was also included.

Also in 1909 Cody's aeroplane – a biplane with a borrowed 50 h.p. Antoinette engine – was nearing success, as were the aeroplanes of Louis Bleriot, who dreamed of flying the English Channel.

Reliable engines with a low weight per horsepower were sought, but either they were too heavy for the power produced, or they were unreliable. Patrick Alexander's prize of £1,000 was won by the Green engine now in the Science Museum.

The book ends with a description of the Cycloplane – a device for fitting to cycles – claimed to give a "certain lifting power when driven through the air". Price three guineas (five guineas superior finish) it was shown at the Aero Exhibition in 1909 by John Gaunt, Aeroplane Engineer of Gargrave, Leeds.

The Motor also published pictures of the Wrights' first glider of 1900 – virtually a kite, with flight to be achieved by a steady head wind or by ropes pulled by an enthusiastic team. If only an engine could be provided to turn a propeller, a pilot would be able to practise. Patrick Alexander achieved this at Windsor by a wind machine blowing towards a tethered glider, but the Camm boys eventually progressed from models to a man carrying glider.

School days and early model aeroplanes

How did it all start in Windsor?

Sydney and F.J.'s father was an excellent carpenter and joiner. A bright scholar, his Great Park school headmaster wanted him to become a school teacher, but money was short in the Camm family, and he was apprenticed at Brown Brothers, the prestigious carriage builders of Windsor, probably for seven years commencing in 1880. By 1887 he was attending night school in Peascod Street and in December of that year he was admitted to the Loyal Magna Charta Lodge of the Independent Order of Odd Fellows.

A skilled workman, he was able to support his growing family. Between 1893 and 1912, twelve children were born in the little two up and two down terrace house, 10 Alma Road, Windsor.

The eldest, Sydney, born August 1893, must have benefited from the expertise and skills of his father, who inculcated interest in handwork, accuracy, and quality. F.J. was born 6th October 1895.

Self-help to knowledge and education was, no doubt, the belief of their parents. What were other factors? Locally there were the experiments at the Imperial Service College, previously United Services College, where Patrick Y. Alexander, an expert balloonist and erstwhile aviator, had presented the College with a workshop with an engine driven fan

The Camm family home at 10 Alma Road, Windsor, (previously 2 Bounty Terrace, Alma Road). The plaque, unveiled by the Mayor on 12th March 1986, commemorates F.J.s elder brother Sydney who earned fame and a knighthood as an aircraft designer for Hawker Siddeley, including the superb Hurricane fighter.

which enabled boys to "pilot" tethered gliders built in the college. No doubt this was generally known in Windsor, and the Camms and their fellows would listen avidly.

Samuel Franklin Cody was flying man carrying kites at Aldershot and at Portsmouth. He and P.Y. Alexander had demonstrated balloons and man carrying kites at Bath in 1903. Cody planned the first British aeroplane. In his article published in 1965, *A Lifetime of Design*, Sydney Camm recorded that his interest in aviation started from seeing in a Windsor model shop, drawings of a model of the WRIGHT biplane published by Messrs Bassett-Lowke. He made a model that was not very successful.

The drawings may have been based upon the Wrights' 1903 application for a patent, which was granted in 1906 – but generally overlooked, until the *Illustrated London News* had drawings made by W.B. Robinson. Sydney's next model was made from drawings published by the *Daily Mail* about the time of Bleriot's memorable flight across the Channel to Dover on 25th July 1909. He spent the next few years making rubber-driven models which led to the formation of the Windsor Model Aeroplane Club.

Before Sydney left the Royal Free School in 1908, aged 14, he spent hours whittling propellers for model aeroplanes. The brothers became sufficiently competent in building reliable model aeroplanes that they supplied to Herberts' Eton High Street shop. Their models of biplanes and monoplanes were advertised as "Will Really Fly", and "Will Rise From The Ground". They found that a better price could be obtained by direct sales to the Eton College boys – these had to be delivered, at night, via a string lowered from the Eton boys' dormitory to avoid notice from the school authorities – and by Herberts, who were not amused to find out what was happening.

For years balloons had been inflated for Guards officers at the Windsor gas works that adjoined the Camm's terrace. In Alma Road Aviation Science was taught by Patrick Y. Alexander to the boys of United Service College, previously known as St Mark's and later as Imperial Service College. Not only was Patrick Alexander wealthy, but he visited the USA where the brothers Wright experimented with gliders and dreamed of powered flight – not that this was thought to be possible. Ornithopters with bird like wings that flapped were thought to be "more practical".

The Wright Brothers aviation news comes to Windsor

Records in the U.S. Airforce Museum, Dayton, Ohio, refer to "Patrick Y. Alexander who visited the Wright family at Dayton and joined their Christmas Eve dinner 24th December 1902" (when the Wrights had only flown gliders, but planned powered flight), also that a year later this was achieved by Wilbur and Orville. On 17th December 1903 at Kitty Hawk North Carolina their aeroplane piloted by Orville remained airborne for 12 seconds and flew a distance of 120 feet. The Wrights thought they were ready to try powered flight in November 1903, and sent a telegram to their designer friend Octave Chanute saying "Yourself and Mr. Alexander welcome after November 5th. Bring abundant bedding". Chanute missed Alexander – who had gone to Blue Hills near Boston to see Dr Graham Bell – and Chanute who was "a bit of a dude" could not stand the primitive living conditions at Kitty Hawk, and returned home. Thus neither Chanute nor Alexander saw the famous flight on 17th December 1903, to their everlasting regret, as P.Y.A. reported to the boys at Windsor. He had reported to the Aeronautical Society of Great Britain concerning the Wrights' progress towards powered flight in America, and was not believed. At that time the Society considered more useful the Report of their Wings Committee about experiments with flapping wings, which had been modelled on the wings of a flying fox. In December 1907 the Society seems to have thought that P.Y.A. was an agent of the United States Government, because the Aero Clubs of America regarded him with affection – he was the only Britisher included in their book "Members of the Aero Clubs of America in Cartoon." (This cartoon is reproduced by courtesy of the Library of Congress, Washington, U.S.A. and the Cross Manufacturing Co. Ltd of Bath).

Patrick Y. Alexander (1867-1943)
Patron and Pioneer of Aeronautics and Aviation
Science teacher at Windsor.
Cartoon by courtesy of the Library of Congress,
Washington, USA and Cross Manufacturing Co. Ltd. (Bath)

"Twelve Seconds to the Moon" (Rosamund Young and Catherine Fitzgerald – a story of the Wright Brothers) includes the reference "Patrick Y. Alexander, an agent for the British Government, made a trip to Dayton in April (1906) and was a dinner guest at the Wright home. The brothers suspected he had come to find out whether they had agreed to sell to the French."

How much of this reached the boys at Windsor, including the Camms is not clear. Certainly P.Y.A. was not a government agent, but an amateur aviation enthusiast who spent his fortune in the interest of British aviation, without much honour. His collection of cuttings from all over the world can be seen in the Science Museum Library, shelf reference B105, Callmark ALEX. They extend from 31st May 1892 to 20th September 1913. They are fragile, most have been microfilmed, and are in about 200 boxes. A readers ticket is required. They are in several languages including French, German, Russian, Italian etc. I found what his name looked like in these languages, and obtained copies for translation when writing P.Y.A.'s biography for the Cross Manufacturing Co of Bath, in 1982-1984.

P.Y.A.'s work as Aviation science teacher at Imperial Service College in Alma Road, Windsor would have needed technical assistants for e.g. propeller, wings and kite making and experiments, which were on a considerable scale, and reported in U.S.A. as well as the U.K. The Camms were close by, and in touch with Eton College boys, and it seems possible that W.M.A.C. members could have helped P.Y.A. with financial advantage to the Club. Unfortunately no records appear to exist in this matter. Research at Dayton was facilitated by the Engineers Club of Dayton following talks given by the writer on 5th and 7th April 1988, accompanied by the late Mr Michael Cross of Bath.

P.Y.A.'s gift of £10,000 to Imperial Service College and the special laboratory he provided for instruction in aviation science in Windsor were famous. He may be the anonymous supporter whose financial help to the W.M.A.C. is known – he was regarded as a "soft touch" where aviation was concerned.

The large fuselage on a horse drawn cart in 1910, St Leonards Road, Windsor

The Wokingham Whale

The *Daily Mail* had offered £1,000 for the first successful flight across the Channel, and this had resulted in many attempts to build a suitable aeroplane. One of these was, according to a *Lloyds Weekly News* illustration dated 9th January 1910, being constructed in Wokingham by a journeyman carpenter, Mr A.M. Farbrother.

A photograph shows a large fuselage on a horse drawn cart outside the entrance to the cemetery, St Leonards Road, at Windsor. It was brought from Wokingham on a Pickford horse and cart, for an 80 h.p. Bleriot engine to be fitted. Photographs inscribed "The Airship gondola" are dated January 1910. The 16 port holes were to hold poles on which canvas was to be spread forming "wings".

At that time Patrick Y. Alexander was a part time aeronautics teacher at the United Services College in Alma Road, Windsor. He was regarded as a propeller design expert, and the Farbrother aircraft was to be "lifted" by power transmitted by a long shaft. P.Y. Alexander kept several cuttings from *Motor World* and *Flight* about the machine, which was seen by many Windsor boys, probably including the Camms.

It was huge, 66 feet long – to be extended to 140 feet – when it was to be 31 feet high and 20 feet wide. Cigar shaped, and telescopic, to have a "Rotoscope" making 1,200 revolutions per minute to lift it into the air, complete with seating, electric lighting, "self-balancing" hammocks, and lavatory accommodation, "for navigation over seas and other waters". Application was made for patents, but these appear to have been refused.

The fuselage was conveyed back to Wokingham, where it was eventually broken up, after Mr Farbrother had sold his cottage to finance the project, helped by donations from Wokingham people. Enthusiasm had outstripped skill and financial prudence again.

The Wokingham Whale outside the entrance to the cemetery, St Leonards Road, Windsor

The Taplow Gyropter

There were rumours of other flying machines being built in the district, one at Maidenhead and another at Taplow between 1910 and 1912. The latter was the dream of Mr George Louis Outram Davidson since 1883, when he began to study bird flight. This led Davidson – and many others – to develop flapping wings, called ornithopters. After experiments with model rotary propeller "lifters", he decided to build a vertical take off air liner to carry passengers intercontinentally. This was before the Wrights had managed powered flight. His huge machine with two great rotary wings never flew. A previous project built in Colorado to be powered by two h.p. Stanley steam engines was destroyed in 1908 when a trial steam engine blew up. Undeterred, Davidson started his Taplow machine project, which was viewed by a Government official, but failed to attract the finance needed for its completion. At least it provided work for a number of craftsmen.

The Benton Air-Car

There is a tenuous connection of the Camms with John F. Benton of Maidenhead and Chalvey by reason of the wheels he donated to the W.M.A.C. and some references to activity at Maidenhead. John Benton was active from 1911 regarding "flying machine undercarriage patents" and in 1915 in connection with a "variable speed tractor biplane". The latter is mentioned on letters from "Green Lane Engineering Works, Bray Road, Maidenhead". They had "Flying grounds at Chalvey near Slough". One letter is addressed to G. Russell-Clarke, Chalvey Wireless Station. J.H. Benton was connected with W. Allen, the manufacturer of cameras at Bray Road, Maidenhead who became a manufacturer of guns and shells. Benton's flying field at Manor Farm, Chalvey and its hangar was sometimes open to the public and was visited by Eton College boys. The Camms could have been aware of Mr Benton's experimental works regarding his "air car". This work had been preceded by models from about 1908, and when these were perfected, Mr Benton secured the services of Mr Allen "to do work in wood, iron and steel" (The Benton

& Allen Story by Jack Turner, 1992). The "air car" crashed in 1911 during a final trial flight attempt ("Final as the field is required for hay".) Benton's patents for using wheels and/or skids are dated 1912, and Sydney certainly expressed a preference for skids.

Later the flying field was used by the Jackaman Brothers (contractors who flew their Moth biplane for early morning sea bathing on the south coast) (*Slough – a Pictorial History*, Judith Hunter and Isobel Thompson).

Benton was known in the Congo as an "Australian engineer who in 1904 installed the first wireless station working between Banana and Ambrizette. He would have been capable of interesting F.J. in wireless. It is not known if F.J. ever visited the wireless station at Chalvey.

The Camms and Aviation

The Camm's garden was bounded by the Royal Windsor Gaslight Works, and the Great Western Railway viaduct adjoined the north end of the short terrace of houses which included number 10 Alma Road, Windsor.

The gas works were used at one time by Guards officers to fill their private balloons, a recreation that continued for several decades in the 19th century. The viaduct sometimes intercepted the Camm brothers' model aeroplanes which young George Camm would be sent round to collect.

Their father had a small workshop shed in the garden, and this was used by the boys for meetings until the Windsor Model Aeroplane Club was started in 1911. They rented a shed nearby in Arthur Road. This was a welcome retreat from the crowded house with its 11 active children – another one had died in infancy.

The rent of the club shed was one shilling and sixpence per week (7½ pence) and this was not always easy to raise, especially when materials for model making had to be bought. The light was by a borrowed hurricane lamp, and paraffin came in a medicine bottle.

The streets were muddy or dusty, surfaced by gravel dredged from the River Thames, and contaminated by horse droppings. The Borough water cart was filled from the pump in Datchet Road, and the boys would play behind the cart, running through the spray. Eton Waterworks did not always allow use by the water cart – there was no reservoir, and the supply relied on river driven pumps. Emergency steam driven pumps had to be stoked up if there was a fire at night, when the river was too high or too low for emergency power.

The Alma Road area was subject to winter flooding from the river, and (as in 1894), these floods could be catastrophic, necessitating the family moving upstairs. Fevers were endemic. "Walking funerals" for a child cost £5 and were all too common.

The children's toys were tops, pea shooters, glass marbles from Codd's lemonade bottles, peg dolls and skipping ropes for the girl, and kites for the boys.

Sydney Camm once said that his interest in aviation started off by his seeing in a Windsor model shop some drawings of the Wright brother's biplane of 1903. These drawings had been published by Messrs Bassett-Lowke, for whom F.J. would write in later years. Sydney made a model which he said was not very successful.

Another model was made from drawings published by the *Daily Mail* after Bleriot's flight across the English Channel to Dover on 25th July 1909. This was the year that Orville Wright went to Germany to teach the Germans how to fly Wright machines.

Cody had made the first powered flight in Britain at Farnborough on 16th October 1908, the same year that Wilbur Wright had amazed the French when he took off and flew at Hunaudieres, where he circled twice without even a preliminary test flight.

In Britain model aeroplane building and flying was preceded by kite flying. The Kite Flying Association of Great Britain had been founded in 1909 with Major Baden Powell as President. He was brother of the Chief Scout, and one of the youngest members of the Aeronautical Society of Great Britain which had been resuscitated by money from P.Y. Alexander about the end of 1897.

In Windsor P.Y. Alexander was giving talks to the boys of United Services College about balloons, kites and aeroplanes at the invitation of the Head Master Mr Nagel. The college was to become Imperial Services College in 1912, when P.Y. Alexander gave several gifts of apparatus to the college where he taught Aviation Science. Later he appears to have helped the Windsor Model Aeroplane Club.

The imagination of local boys regarding aerial flight was stimulated by the books they could get on loan from the Albert Institute Library of the Windsor & Eton Literary Scientific and Mechanics Institution. Mr W. Fairbanks was librarian. There were powerful stories such as "The Clipper of the Clouds" by Jules Verne and "The War In The Air" written in 1908 by H.G. Wells (once an apprentice in Windsor). Wells wrote about the German attack on New York in a gigantic effort for world supremacy using airships developed from the Zeppelins of 1905/6. "How War Came To New York" described the first bombs dropped on a city as imagined by H.G. Wells.

The facts of Bleriot's flight in 1909 above the greatest battleships and double the speed of the fastest steamers amazed almost everyone and H.G. Wells wrote in the *Daily Mail* "I could imagine the day of reckoning coming like a swarm of birds".

Journals such as "Boy's Own Paper" were provided by P.Y. Alexander to the college, and these included articles on kite flying, model aircraft, and even a man carrying glider. In due course F.J. would write for the "B.O.P.".

Flight – The "Weekly journal about Aerial Locomotion and Transport" – was published every Thursday – a day looked forward to by Sydney in particular and all the boys who formed the Windsor Model Aeroplane Club.

The cost was one penny. F.J. had one shilling (5p) per week as an apprentice during his first year. Sydney being in his third year would have had perhaps three shillings. Founded in 1909 *Flight* was the official organ of the Aero Club of the United Kingdom – not yet the Royal Aeronautical Society. It was superseded by *The Aeroplane*, edited by C.G. Grey in 1911, and Sydney recorded his deep appreciation of the enormous contribution to the progress of aviation in Great Britain by these journals. He wrote "They stimulated thought and aroused the enthusiasm of the younger generation".

The older generation tended to be less enthusiastic, and even horrified at the prospect of powered flight, and discouraged the practice of gliding with its necessity for towing the machines by ropes pulled – in Windsor – by boys. *Flight* recorded successful gliding experiments and published photographs in (sometimes) poor quality half tone blocks – including the "troubles from which lessons are learnt" i.e. crashes. It claimed to be the "First Aero Weekly in the World".

The First Flights to Windsor in 1911

In February 1911 Mr T.O.M. Sopwith flew to Windsor, landing first at Datchet to visit his sister, as fog barred the route to Windsor Castle where he was due to land before the King. He circled the Round Tower – a feat that Sydney vowed to repeat – then landed on the lawns near the Castle for an inspection by George V and Queen Mary with their sons. Windsor and Eton boys hurried to see the wonder, and it was announced that prizes were to be given for the best model of Sopwith's aeroplane. Sydney won second prize. Twelve years later he would become Tommy Sopwith's chief designer of aeroplanes.

In 1953 Sir Thomas Sopwith and Sir Sydney Camm were both awarded knighthoods in the Coronation Honours list, and they were photographed together. Near contemporaries, they were miles apart in their upbringing and social backgrounds.

In September 1911 came the Coronation Aerial Post from Hendon to Windsor. This had been arranged by Sir Walter Windham, and was a most exciting event for all the boys of the area. Permission had been granted by the Deputy Ranger Sir Walter Campbell for a landing ground on the Review Ground, Windsor

T.O.M. Sopwith on the East Lawn at Windsor Castle, 1st February 1911, a flight made at the request of The King.

Great Park. In the event, Gustav Hamel came down in the meadow between Frogmore Mausoleum and the Long Walk.

These flights were reviewed in *Flight*, and more and more local boys became makers of model aeroplanes. Sydney and F.J. Camm resolved to form a model aeroplane club, and early in 1912 the first meetings were held in the garden shed at 10 Alma Road.

On Saturday, 9th September 1911, Gustav Hamel took off from Hendon in a Bleriot monoplane landing in Shaw Farm Meadow, near the Frogmore Mausoleum, Windsor. Thus a great advance in postal delivery was inaugurated in which Windsor played a central role.

Further flights were made carrying mail in either direction until 25th September.

The Windsor aerial posting box used to be kept in the Guildhall Exhibition; it is now in the Corporation Depot Windsor Collection store with some of the cards that were carried. The Golden Jubilee of this event was held in Windsor on 9th September 1961. A helicopter duplicated the first flight again from Hendon, a special mail was carried, and an Exhibition of Air Mail stamps was held in the Guildhall, followed by a celebration dinner at the Thames Hotel at which Lord Samuel (Postmaster General in 1911), who promoted the First Airmail Flight, made a memorable speech.

Driver's Arrival in Windsor Great Park with the second aeroplane. Gustav Hamel flew the first aeroplane.

Two Windsor boys – F.J. Camm and A.W. Mainwood are said to be between the policeman and the lady next to a girl with a hoop.

The penny magazine that Sydney Camm and all the members of his Windsor Aero Club read avidly every week. Sydney sent in monthly reports of their activities.

The Windsor Model Aeroplane Club is formed in 1911

Guided by reports of other clubs in *Flight*, Sydney and F.J. arranged for local boys to co-operate extolling the advantages of a club workshop and local and other competitions including those arranged by Mr G.A. Broomfield of Aldershot. Mr Broomfield was in touch with Cody, and claimed to meet famous people such as Sir Hiram Maxim, Wilbur and Orville Wright, A.V. Roe, Grahame-White, Sir Geoffrey de Havilland as well as T.O.M. Sopwith. Mr Broomfield recorded being impressed by "two very remarkable young men from Windsor – Sydney and Fred Camm, one destined to design the Hurricane aeroplane, which by winning the Battle of Britain prevented Great Britain from becoming a German colony, the other to become a great editor of technical journals and books on engineering in all its branches". (Quote from his *Pioneer of the Air*.)

The club premises was a shed in Arthur Road, Windsor, a stone's throw from 10 Alma Road. The rent was one shilling and sixpence per month (7½p). It had no lighting – this resulted in an oil lamp being scrounged, plus a medicine bottle of paraffin. The members were photographed in the yard adjoining the club, including F.J. Camm, S. Barton, Sydney Camm, A.W. Mainwood, J. Saunders, F. Stevenson, E. (Ginger) Stanbrook and R. Clayton. There were other members including Hendry – the son of the builder Sydney had been apprenticed to – and J.G. Starnes of Maidenhead – who sometimes brought his sister to watch the models being flown, and provided an alternative site at their home. Sydney was to marry Hilda Starnes at Christmas, 1915. Charles Camm was one of the "pilots" when a man carrying glider was built in 1913 – and George Camm was used to retrieve "lost" models from the railway viaduct, and to buy Japanese silk from the dress materials shop in Peascod Street, to his great embarrassment, at the age of 12 years.

Sydney reported the club's progress to *Flight*, including their competitions with Aldershot at Long Valley. These were every Wednesday and Sunday during the summer. F.J. wrote the reports when Sydney was working away from Windsor with Martinsyde at Brooklands. The club site is now marked with a plaque in Ward Royal. Competition rules required that timed flights be from launch to landing – or until the time a flight passed out of sight. This was the fate of several models, including one of F.J.'s in August 1914. They were surprised to read that duration flights in Australia and the U.S.A. were much longer than in the U.K. and it was found that the air currents and wide open spaces abroad permitted longer glides. The Windsor club members made up to three models each per week, but crashes were frequent, and Sydney was unable to send detailed reports of all of them for inclusion in *Flight*.

The last surviving member, Bob Mainwood, grandson of a William Street, Windsor mineral water bottler, used to tell stories about the club, its successes and failures, with a gusto that lost nothing in the telling. Members with bicycles used to go to see "real" aeroplanes flying, including the French pilot Peygoud "Loop the Loop" and perform inverted flying. This feat was also performed by Hamel above Windsor Castle to impress the King.

The elder Camm boys would cycle to Hendon to see the flying. In 1913 a famous London Underground poster by Tony Sarg illustrated in vibrant colour Graham White's pusher biplane of wood, wire and canvas passing above the boundary beacons which marked the turning points to be navigated.

Models became more sophisticated, and Sydney and F.J. began to plan a man carrying glider. Sydney dreamed of fitting an engine so that they could fly around the Round Tower of Windsor Castle, as Sopwith had done in 1911. The materials are listed in F.J.'s Mss (printed in 1919). The first list used bamboo ("135 yards of 1¼ inch in lengths 6, 14 and 19 feet") also 175 yards of piano wire, .056 inch diameter (17 S.W.G.), 7 feet of 3/16th inch copper tube to make rigging eyes – 9 dozen were needed, 25 yards of double width calico, one square yard of 24 gauge brass sheet, a gross of 1 inch ³⁄₁₆ inch screws and nuts and a ball of cord". All the tools required were "hand-pliers, hacksaw, and a wood saw", with varnish also starch paste to shrink the calico. The cost totalled £3. They found that spruce was better than bamboo. Sydney found an engine advertised for £25 that had been purchased from A.V. Roe by Miss Bland of Belfast. It was 1914, then war intervened. Their glider was broken up in 1919.

Extract from 'Flight' dated September 3rd, 1915
'The Loading etc., of Models:-'

"In some notes regarding the work of the Windsor Model Aero Club which have been sent by Mr. F.J. Camm, there are the following which will doubtless prove helpful to some other readers of this section:-

"From a résumé of the majority of duration machines constructed by members, I find that a loading of four ounces per square foot has given by far the best results. Indeed, models which are loaded under this margin have revealed a point which has manifested itself on several occasions latterly to the writer; it is that models loaded at three ounces per square foot have not given such good results as those loaded at four ounces. The former have without exception given much trouble in the adjustment of the centre of pressure, and requiring weather conditions as nearly as possible ideal.

"A biplane is altogether a more interesting model to build, for it presents interesting constructional problems, which are lacking in the majority of monoplanes, while however simple may be its construction it certainly evades the term 'flying stick.' Quite apart from this, however, there is the increased amount of theoretical problems entailed, such as the correct position for the centre of thrust, thus requiring a deeper study of those laws which need to be only partly known to fly an A frame. Most of the members of this club have found that the centre of thrust placed slightly above the centre of greatest resistance has given best results with biplanes, while an overhang on the top plane effects good lateral stability. A camber of one-twelfth the chord has been found to be ample for models up to twelve ounces.

"In many of the early tractors constructed by members, the rubber its the centre of thrust) was placed underneath the spar, but difficulty of adjusting the centre of pressure with the thrust low was experienced, so that it was ultimately placed above the motor rod. A much lower ratio of areas was employed than with canards, indeed I think this an essential for longitudinal stability. From experiments conducted by the members, the most effective position of the rudder was above the thrust line, much better stability and directional control being manifest than with its area equally disposed about the model's centre line of thrust. No angle of incidence was used, or found necessary, on the main surfaces of their tractor machines, the longitudinal vee for stabilising purposes being maintained by a negative angle of 3° approx. on the tail. Better flying qualities have also resulted from models having a Morane wing area."

The first man carrying glider was completed and flown in 1913 – with younger brother Charlie Camm occupying the position as "Pilot" – and instructed not to touch the controls. Another flight – with Ginger Stanbrook as pilot – crash landed, breaking Ginger's collarbone. (He related this incident when a member of the Windsor Rescue Party (ARP) during the 1939-45 war).

In 1914, the engine acquired from erstwhile aviatrix Miss Bland of Belfast was being fitted. But first it had to be tested.

It arrived at Windsor from Ireland, and one Sunday the club members took it through 10 Alma Road and into the shed in the back garden. It was bolted to the workbench, and – still dressed in their Sunday best, complete with straw hats – they took turns to swing the propeller. Suddenly it started with an unsilenced roar, which ruined the peace of that quiet Sunday afternoon.

Although claimed to be "balanced" the vibration caused the heavy work bench to "walk" around the shed. The flailing propeller sent wood shavings – and straw hats – flying. The propeller made it difficult to stop the engine, which eventually stopped. The uproar brought the police, who gave the culprits a stiff warning. No one was any the better for being sprayed with oil.

The engine was taken to the club hut, but the outbreak of war in 1914 intervened, and the work was never completed. For some reason the rent of the hut was overdue, and the landlord padlocked the door to prevent access. George Camm cut through the brickwork, removed the precious engine and tools, and rebuilt the wall, so that the landlord could never understand what had happened.

By this time Sydney was working for Martinsyde at Brooklands – he had married in 1915 – and F.J. flew model aeroplanes for the castle guard to aim at.

After F.J. left school in 1910, he was apprenticed by his father to Brown Brothers, the prestigious coachbuilders of Frances Road, Windsor. Here his father had been an apprentice before him. Apprenticeship was for seven years.

Only the best was good enough for Browns. The eldest son Walter became managing director, Augustus ran the blacksmith's shop, Arthur the body maker, Leon the trimmer, while Robert was in

George Camm with the Cowley Aero Engine, "recovered from an Irish Bog" and advertised in *Flight* (about 1912) and bought from Miss Bland of Belfast by Sydney Camm for £25 for W.M.A.G.C. Some parts were missing, however, and they were made and replaced by a friend Mr W.H. Deller of D.S.S. Engineering, 60, Alma Road, Windsor.

charge of painting – including the Lord Mayor's coach in London. There were about 60 employees, and F.J. could gain experience of the high class work undertaken. Browns had a valuable export trade with sultans and maharajas ordering luxury work.

Part of the property was leased to D.S. Fitch Motor Works, who hired out luxurious Sizaire cars. These originated in France, and the chassis were driven to the channel ports and brought to England for the best bodywork to be fitted. This was mainly done by firms such as Windovers in Bond Street, but some may have been done in Windsor. Fitches eventually became A.A. Clarks of Windsor.

The finished cars were indistinguishable from Rolls Royce, even to having identical radiators except for the name label. This eventually caused Rolls Royce to take action against Sizaire – which Rolls Royce lost, as Sizaires had patented the design, and Rolls Royce had not done so, an omission that cost them £25,000.

It is said that seen across the road the Sizaires were identical in appearance with Rolls Royce cars. F.J. copied the luxurious buttoned leather finish for the seat he built for the club gliders, using rare duraluminium framing.

Gamages and Benetfinks of Cheapside included model aeroplanes and what was termed "Wireless Telegraphy" in their early catalogues, as well as motor cycles, cameras and other factory built goods that the Camms could not afford. The boys had impressed the *Windsor Express*, as reported in the edition dated 15th November 1913:-

WINDSOR AERO CLUB.

RULES AND SUBSCRIPTION CARD.

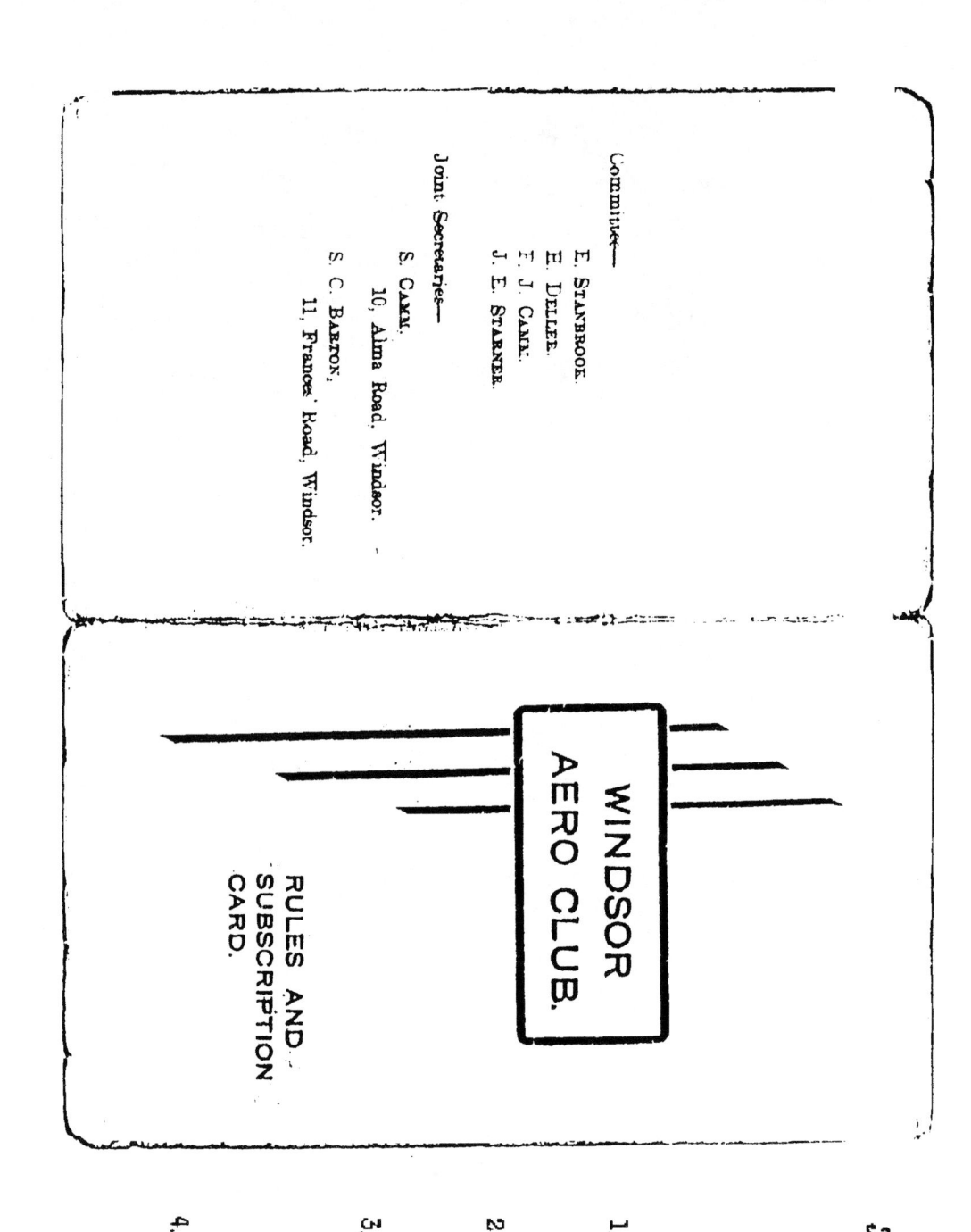

Name..................................

RULES.

1.—The subscription shall be 1/2 per month payable on the first Saturday in each month.

2.—The Workshops will be available for Members from 6 p.m., Saturdays 2.30 p.m., and Sundays.

3.—Monthly Competitions will be organised by the Committee for the Members' Challenge Cup, which will become the property of any Member winning the competition three times.

4.—The Committee hold the power to amend or alter these rules.

Committee—
 E. STANBROOK.
 E. DELEE.
 F. J. CANN.
 J. E. STARNER.

Joint Secretaries—
 S. CANN,
  10, Alma Road, Windsor.
 S. C. BARTON,
  11, Frances Road, Windsor.

This is the first club card as arranged by Sydney

Windsor Aero Club members. Sydney Camm is standing, second from left, and F.J. Camm is standing third from right.

Windsor Aero Club
(from the Windsor Express, 15th November 1913)

A Correspondent writes: "As mentioned in your last issue, there is a club in Windsor which has for its object the furthering of the science of Aeronautics. The club was founded by Mr. S. Camm, now the secretary, about three years ago, since when a vast amount of progress has been made. The early experiments were executed with models, of which many different kinds were made. A good flying model is intensely interesting, as it produces in exact miniature the flight of real aeroplanes, and it is not surprising that the flying of these has always attracted attention. Even an ordinary rubber driven model is an intricate piece of work, as the rules to be observed are the same as hold good in full size design. In February this year the club exhibited models at the Aero Show at Olympia, and were very favourably commented upon by the Press. It is interesting to recall that the King personally inspected the models and expressed a wish to see them fly. Shortly after, Mr. S. Camm competed at Hendon, coming in third. Having progressed so far, it was felt that the experiments should take a more ambitious line, so the construction and flying of gliders was begun. A glider is an aeroplane without the engine, and is operated similarly to a man-lifting kite. The machine is towed against the wind, until it attains a certain height, when the ropes are released, and the machine glides down. Of course much better results can be gained by gliding off the top of a hill or other eminence, but this entails a certain amount of risk. It will thus be seen that it is possible to experience a few of the joys of flying without the expense of an engine.

"Their first machine was a biplane of 32ft. span, and a great many glides were made, until after many vicissitudes it was completely wrecked. Almost at once a second machine was started, and when finished was exhibited at the Royal Counties' Show. It is with this machine that the club is now experimenting. It is considered one of the best gliders in the country, a decided tribute to the abilities of the club. It is the intention of the club to enter on the final phase, which is the building of an engine-driven machine, which, should it materialise, would fully justify the trouble taken.

The original photograph of the W.M.A. & G. Club glider used by
Sydney Camm in his book *Aeroplane Construction*.
F.J. used the same picture for his book *The Design of Model Aeroplanes*,
Chapter XXI, "Building a Glider", page 163.

That they are capable of the work is quite apparent to anyone seeing their specimens. Of course the expenses would be increased enormously, and as up to the present the club has been entirely self-supporting, some extra financial help will be required. It must be understood that the projected machine will be on strictly orthodox lines, as, up to now, experimental machines have not met with much success.

"All those interested in aviation are invited to join, or any rate to pay a visit to the workshop in Arthur Road any evening in the week. The Secretary's address is 10, Alma Road, Windsor."

A heavily touched-up photograph of "The Glider in the Air" (with no pilot)
dated Oct 4th 1913, appeared in 'Flight'.

A faded glimpse into the early days. This is a 1912 picture of Windsor Model Aero and Gliding Club's original members in the workshop yard at Arthur Road, Windsor. From left: F.J. Camm (brother of the founder), S. Barton, Sir Sydney Camm, A.W. Mainwood, Saunders, F. Stevenson, Stanbrook, R. Clayton.

The W.M.A. Club second glider on display at Windsor Home Park in 1913, Royal Agricultural Show.

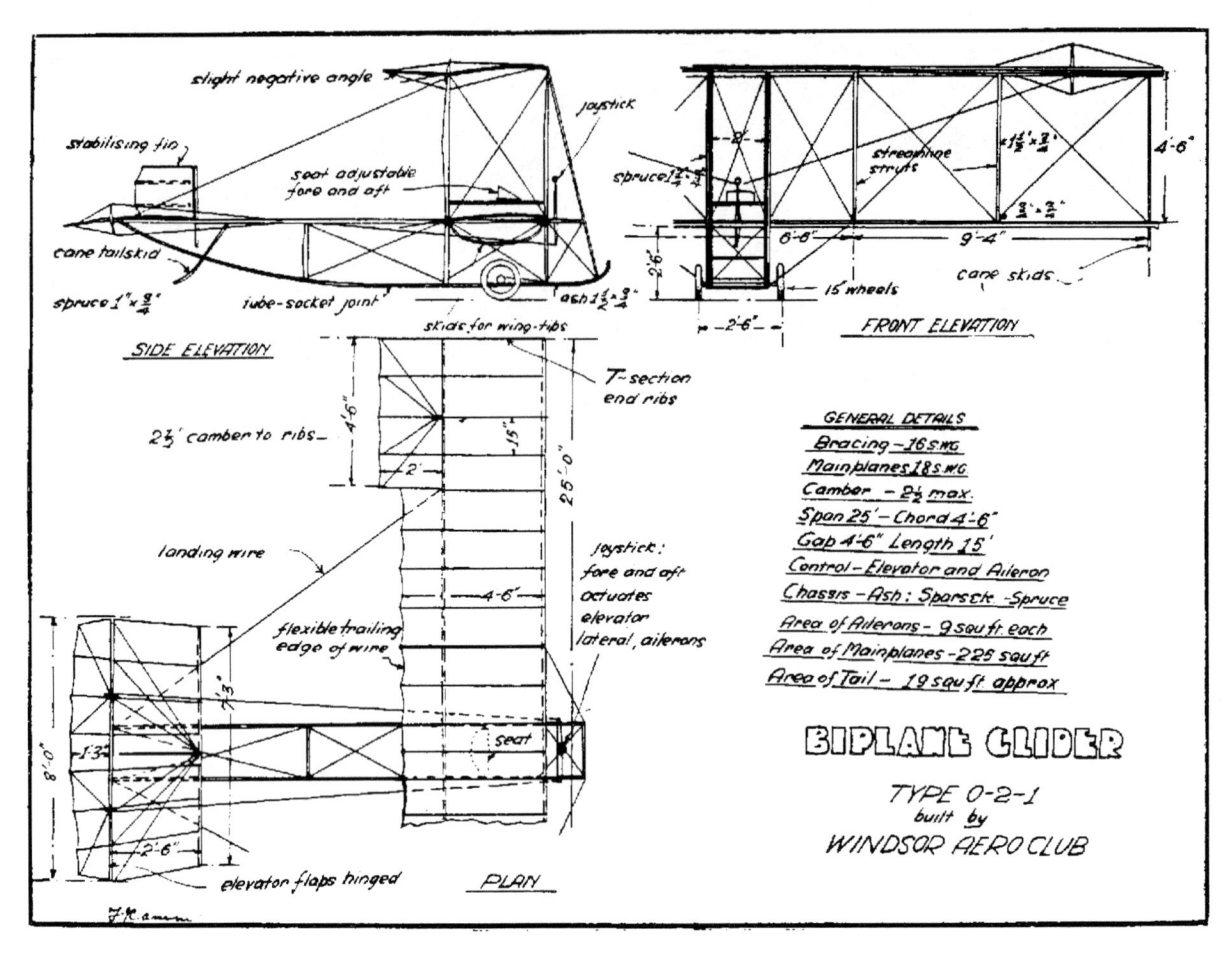

Elevations and plan of W.M.A.C. Glider published in Every Day Science, October, 1922

The Windsor Model Aeroplane Club

Sydney Camm in his book *Aeroplane Construction*, written in 1914 before the war developed and not published until 1919, described the "low-powered tractor biplane which was completed except for the covering by the Windsor Model Aeroplane Club". He included a photograph. The Club had changed its name to The Windsor Model Aeroplane and Glider Club (W.M.A.G.C.) to celebrate their work.

In 1919, F.J. Camm published his book *The Design of Model Aeroplanes* in the Benn Brothers 'Aeronautics' series. This had a second edition in which he was stated to be "Model Editor of *Flight*, Technical Editor *Everyday Science*, etc etc". Both editions had a Foreword by Mr Handley Page – one of the pioneer airmen members of the Aero Models Association of 1909 listed by Alex Houlberg in his *"50 years of modelling"* (dated March 1959 in *Aeromodeller*).

Chapter XXI, "Building a Glider" (pages 146-165) includes illustrations Figs. 132-154 of details, and a photograph "An Interesting Biplane Glider". F.J. referred to this glider – or perhaps one or another of the three built – in *Everyday Science* and included "Framework of the Glider built by Mr F.J. Camm" and repeated the photograph of the "Completed Glider", March 1920.

Again in *Everyday Science* in April 1922 he refers to the "W.A.C. Biplane" and included a photograph of "the front portion of the 25 h.p. biplane built by the Windsor Aero Club. The engine is an early – horizontally – opposed two stroke". (page 668).

A further page appeared on page 376 of *Everyday Science* dated October 1922 with Elevations and plan of the W.M.A.C. Glider on page 377.

Two Camm marriages, and F.J. becomes Editor for Everyday Science

The first to leave home was Sydney, who gave his address as Bourne End when he married at Christmas 1915 to Hilda Rose Starnes, sister of one of the W.M.A. Club members. Her family lived at Bourne End – where the club sometimes flew models, and one of the big gliders. The wedding at the Parish Church Wooburn was attended by the couples' fathers, Ernest Temple Starnes, confectioner, and Frederick William Camm, Joiner.

Sydney stated in 1915 that he was an aeroplane mechanic. He had started life on leaving school in 1908 as an apprentice to Hendry, of Butcher & Hendry Builders, Grove Road, Windsor, leaving in 1914 for "war work" with Martinsyde at Brooklands. It was not long before he was promoted to the drawing office, but this is not the history of Sydney, whose biography in detail can be found in Dr John Fozard's *Sydney Camm and the Hurricane*. In 1919 F.J. lived at 53 Grove Road, Windsor and Bob Mainwood who was to become the last survivor of the W.M.A.C. recalled seeing him running for the train from Windsor to London clutching his lunch case and papers. When F.J. married Dorothy May Field, age 18, of 58 Park Street, Slough on 6th April 1919 he gave his address as 32 Old Change, London, EC1, and his occupation as "Engineer". This address is under the shadow of St Pauls. The marriage at St Lawrence Upton-cum-Chalvey was attended by his eldest sister, Edith Florence Camm, then aged 21 – she became Mrs Alderman of Huddersfield – and Stanley Wade Keeble, his Best Man.

They lived for many years at 53 Grove Road, Windsor where their only son Frederick William Sydney was born on 20th September 1920. He became known as "Little Fred".

F.J. acquired a job with Pitmans in London, where his draughtsmanship and technical writing won him recognition. His interests included bicycle rallies and road racing. He wrote for *Models, Railways and Locomotion*, also *Everyday Science*. He described in *Everyday Science* the W.M.A.C. pre-war biplane man carrying glider and many model aeroplanes. He started on wireless telegraphy and modelling for *Hobbies* and accumulated material for *Practical Wireless* and *Practical Mechanics*. These became the first of *Newnes Practical* series of journals. For recreation, he seems to have enjoyed mass start road racing on bicycles.

In the early days of F.J. Camm's writings, great effort – which was badly paid – was necessary to keep e.g. *Model Engineering* and *Everyday Science* afloat. F.J. supplied material to Henry Greenly. He was a leading figure in Edwardian days, particularly in small scale model railways but was also interested in aeromodelling. Greenly commented that "with twelve hours work a day with aeroplanes I find little time for the paper or for correspondence". During the 1914-18 war, contributions were received from people who found relief from war time conditions by modelling.

Aeroplane crashes were all too common and F.J. noted one that occurred in 1913. On 30th August a Royal Flying Corps machine flying from Hendon towards Maidenhead while flying over Windsor "there was a sudden explosion and the peculiar droning noise made by the propeller ceased". The press report shows that a "Breguet military plane crashed at Bray after engine failure and one of the passengers, Mr De Havilland, was trapped by engine pipes".

Mr Stickland, Borough Engineer at Windsor – whose depot in Alma Road, Windsor was a stone's throw from the Camm's house – after being given a short flight at Hendon about the time of the first (1911) aerial post, and on seeing a pile of wreckage, was told that "this was one of the aeroplanes that had taken part in the Windsor service".

The Camms and the 1914-18 Great War years, and F.J. starts work as a Technical Writer

By 1914 twelve Camm children had been born at 10 Alma Road, Windsor. One died as a baby. F.J. had moved by 1919 to 53 Grove Road, the year he married Dorothy May Field of Slough. Until 1917 F.J. was an apprentice at Brown Brothers.

In Sydney's absence he wrote the W.M.A.C. reports to *Flight* but these seem to end after 1915. He flew model aeroplanes for the Windsor Castle Guard to practise aiming their rifles.

In 1915 the army needed over 30,000 men between 19 and 41 to volunteer each week if conscription was to be avoided. Sydney and F.J. were "starred" men in reserved occupations, initially munitions and coal mining, the railways and war industries.

On 9th January 1915 the Kaiser gave the German naval staff permission to bomb Britain "avoiding London and private dwellings" but 23 Zeppelin air raids had killed 181 people in London and injured 405 others. One Zeppelin was heard far up the Thames – the L13 – before turning south and dropping 18 bombs on Croydon. Dubbed the "Baby Killer", the coroner would not accept the jury verdict of "wilful murder". He did accept a verdict of "Death due to fragments of a bomb thrown from a hostile aircraft". The tremendous noise of the great engines had been unmistakable, and there was alarm at the virtual absence of defence against the monsters, until in September 1916 Second Lieutenant Sowery managed to fire an incendiary bullet into the L32 which crashed near Billericay. Previously British aircraft tried without success to climb above the Zeppelins and hit them with small bombs – but these added to the danger on the ground. Then Gotha bomber raids increased east of Windsor. During this period F.J.'s knowledge and practice of craft skills continued, and he became a capable writer on technical matters. He completed his illustrated Mss for his first book *The Design of Model Aircraft* which was to be published in 1919 by Benn Brothers Ltd., "Aeronautics" offices, 8 Bouverie Street, EC4 with its Foreword by the eminent aeroplane magnate Mr Handley Page. By this time he was accepted as a well known contributor to the technical press on aeronautical matters. A second edition quickly followed, in which F.J. could add that he was "Model Editor of *Flight* and Technical Editor of *Everyday Science*. As can be seen from the long list at the end of this book, his output of technical books steadily increased. The approval of Mr Handley Page was no light matter – he was lecturer in aeronautical matters at the Northampton Polytechnic Institute at Clerkenwell, and a leading figure in aviation and modelling.

F.J. had become familiar with workshop processes at Browns, and could appreciate the need for information and tuition. He wrote accordingly and freelanced for Pitman, Pearson, Cassells and for Henry Greenly, the narrow gauge railway expert. F.J. saw the need for clear simple language and illustrations to teach the facts and enable problems to be overcome. He became familiar with the work of the National Physics Laboratory at Teddington regarding watches – and possibly aerofoil design. His "Camm" five cylinder compressed air model aeroplane engine required a good knowledge of engineering.

F.J.'s five cylinder engine appears in both *Everyday Science*, April 1922 and *Model Aeroplanes* (chapter XIII). He also included a three cylinder engine stated to be based upon a very early French engine.

The Camms celebrated the return of their younger brother Charlie from the 1914-18 war, in which he was wounded at the Battle of the Somme. Charlie had piloted the biplane glider built by the W.M.A.C. before the crash landing when Ginger Stanbrook broke his collar bone and arm. Charlie had started work with the *Windsor Express* in 1914, and eventually completed 50 years of service.

Fig. 178.—Side Elevation

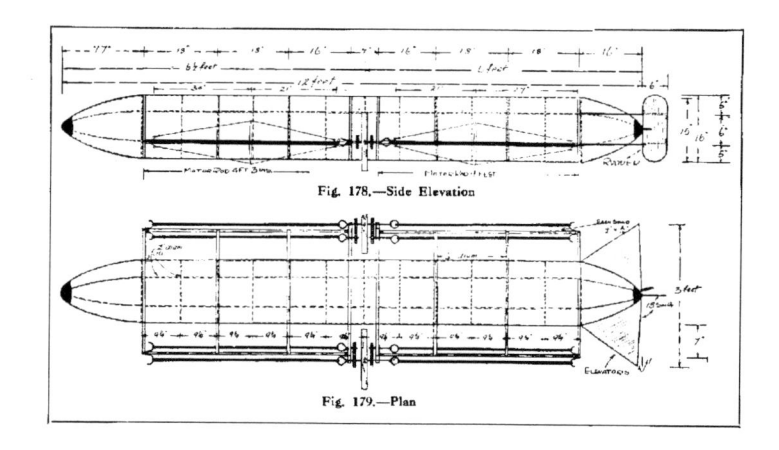

Fig. 179.—Plan

F.J.'s Model Airship plan and Model Airship "In Flight"

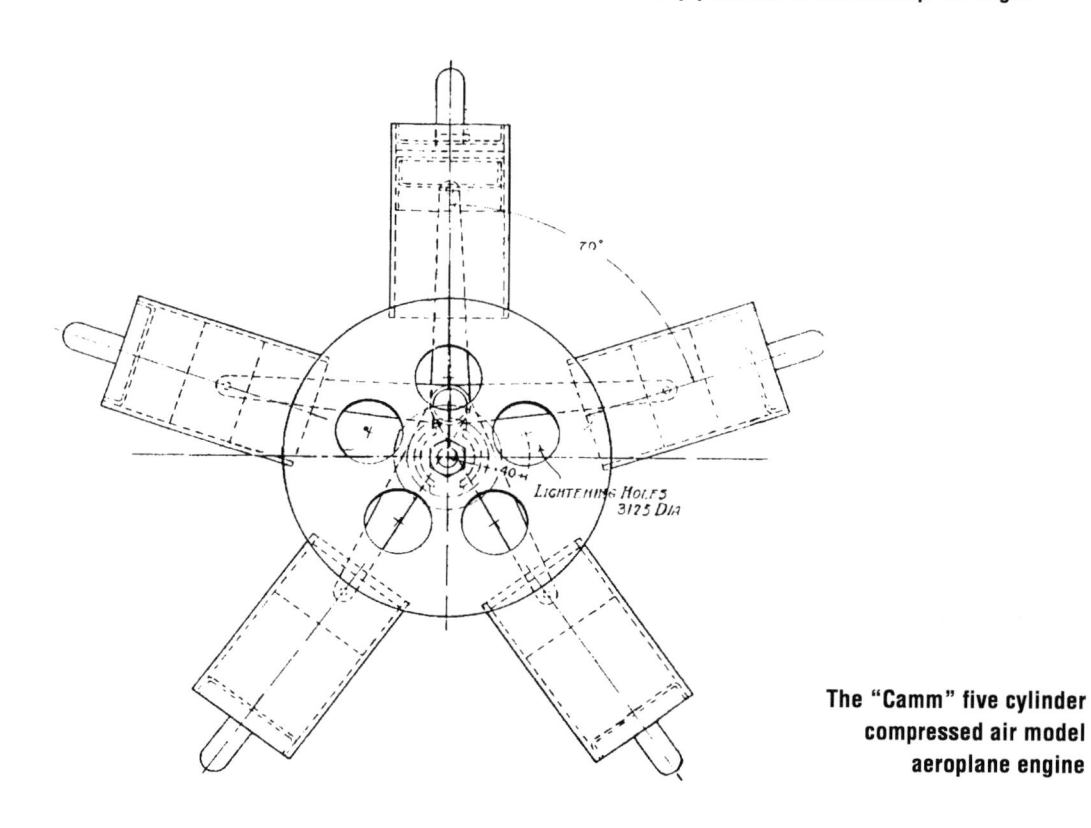

The "Camm" five cylinder compressed air model aeroplane engine

LONG DISTANCE MONOPLANE

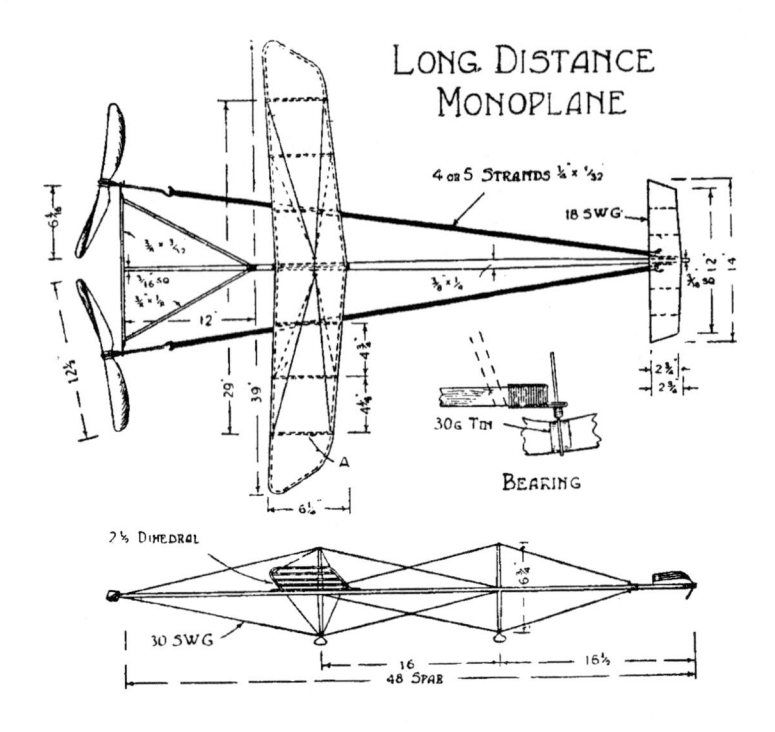

The above illustration dated June 1918, "A Model Monoplane type 1-1-P2," is the first illustration F.J. used in *Models, Railways and Locomotives*.

Soon after F.J.'s wedding in 1919, a tank arrived at the GWR goods yard. It was 29th May 1920 and the ponderous monster with its machine guns, bullet holes and service scars was driven along Arthur Road shaking the Camm's house. At the junction with Alma Road, it turned south from Arthur Road as far as New Road – now Clarence Road – then left towards Bachelors Acre where the reception party – and bands – awaited. Here it remained a feature for 20 years, where the local children played until it was surrounded by iron fencing. On his way to work in London, F.J. was to pass the monster every day for several years.

By 1918 he had acquired a reputation as a technical writer including articles for Henry Greenly's *Models, Railways and Locomotives*. His regular feature under the heading "Model Flying Machines" commenced in June 1918, the writer being recorded as F.J. Camm, MAeS. This journal merged with the new *Everyday Science* published by W. Hansard & Co. F.J. became the "Model Editor Aeronautics" with a postal address for queries, "The Editor, Model Flying Machines, 37-38 Strand, WC." This became a free feature in all

---

The Home Mechanic Series

1/- each net
(By post 1/2)

This series of practical handbooks is designed to answer the questions of the amateur mechanic or craftsman. Each volume is clearly written by an expert and copiously illustrated.

Six new titles :—
11. LATHE WORK FOR AMATEURS.
12. HOUSE DECORATING AND PAINTING.
13. WORKSHOP ARITHMETIC.
14. DOMESTIC PLUMBING.
15. POWER DRIVEN MODEL AIRCRAFT.
16. THE HOME ELECTRICIAN.

ACCUMULATORS.
MOTOR-CAR UPKEEP AND OVERHAUL.
THE HOME WOODWORKER.
MODEL AEROPLANES AND AIRSHIPS.
25 SIMPLE WORKING MODELS
THE HANDYMAN'S ENQUIRE WITHIN.
SIMPLE ELECTRICAL APPARATUS AND EXPERIMENTS.
MODEL BOAT BUILDING.
TOYMAKING FOR AMATEURS.
25 TESTED WIRELESS CIRCUITS.

sale at all Newsagents and Bookstalls, or by post from
GEORGE NEWNES Ltd., 8-11 Southampton Street, Strand, London, W.C.2

Model Aeroplanes and Airships

With Special Chapters on
Gliders, Helicopters, Wing-flapping Models, Kites, and Full-size Gliding

By F. J. CAMM

WITH 120 ILLUSTRATIONS

LONDON
GEORGE NEWNES, LIMITED
SOUTHAMPTON STREET, STRAND, W.C.2

F.J.'s journals thereafter, subject to a stamped addressed envelope – and sometimes a coupon to be cut from the journal. His work appeared in *Everyday Science* until October 1923, when the journal included a "Notice to All Readers" that publication was suspended "owing to prevailing conditions".

The detailed drawings for this monoplane were included in his book *The Design of Model Aeroplanes* (1919) with 12 pages of instructions and illustrations (Figs 46 to 61).

With modifications, it became "A Long Distance Monoplane" (Fig. 61B) pages 75-76 in this book. I think it appears again in *Model Aeroplanes* published by Cassells and Co. In 1921 the latter had published *Mechanical Drawing* edited by B.E. Jones "with our technical editors F.J. Camm and Mr Henry Greenly". These were part of Cassells' Workshop series.

The original George Newnes *Home Mechanic Model Aeroplanes and Airships* book of 1920(?) illustrated 15 or so model aeroplanes dating from 1909, kites, hydro-monoplanes capable of rising from the water (these had been popular with the W.M.A.C.) and an airship. In Cassell's "Work" handbook, *Model Aetroplanes*, by F.J., his was about 13 feet long and 3 feet in diameter – the "actual envelope being 16 inches diameter if hydrogen is used" with four elastic motor twin screws. He gave a list of factors which could render such constructions unsuccessful. These include loss of gas by percolation and substandard quality "gas jet" hydrogen compared with that used by balloon manufacturers. He warned of risk of fire or explosion. The "Camm" bentwood birch screw propeller is detailed.

F.J. commenced his June 1918 *Everyday Science* series by describing the theoretical and practical application of the laws of flight, and his "Practical" approach can be traced from this period. When writing for *Everyday Science*, he sometimes used the pseudonym "Jay Cee" on various subjects – even the weather. Notes about model aeroplanes were followed by improvising workshop tools (as seen later in *Practical Mechanics* from 1933) and there is the first mention of Wireless broadcasting. This increasingly occupied his attention in 1923.

His columns "Amateur Wireless conducted by experts" resulted in his engagement to broadcast from the London station 2LO in June 1922, but no record of his talk has been found. Similarly he had columns in *Hobbies* by 1930, as will be seen in the session dealing with wireless. This started with his regular feature "Practical Wireless Supplement" leading to *Practical Wireless* being started by George Newnes on 24th September 1932.

After *Everyday Science* ceased in 1923, F.J. continued to write for Pitman and other publishers including *Hobbies*. He used the Author's Foreword of the latter to publicise his two publications *Model Aeroplanes and Airships* and *Power-Driven Model Aircraft* (George Newnes Home Mechanic Series, one shilling each (5p).

F.J. first referred to Balsa Wood in *Everyday Science*, March 1921 as being "only obtainable direct from America." A letter addressed to him dated 1922 states that supplies could be obtained from The American Balsa Wood Co, 50E, 42nd Street, New York, U.S.A. in pieces 3 inches x 6 inches x 6 feet "at about ten shillings (50p) the piece". Balsa Wood was later first imported by W.E. Evans, Treasurer of the S.M.A.E., F.J.'s old friend.

F.J.'s *Model Aeroplanes and Airshops*, price one shilling, with its 96 pages including index and illustrations was good value in those days (c. 1930). F.J.'s preface acknowledged his indebtedness to contemporary model makers including S.J. Garratt, H.W. Austin and A. Gunner – and even those sold by Mr A.E. Jones.

In later years, when in 1949 he published his *Model Aeroplane Handbook* (George Newnes, 12 shillings and 6d, 61.25p), *Aeromodeller's* review by C.S.R., May 1949, was critical. The latter seems to have mixed half bricks with his bouquets:–

Model Aeroplane Handbook, by F. J. Camm. (George Newnes, Ltd., 12/6).

Coming from the pen of such a well-known author, many people interested in model aeronautics will be inclined to take this book as authoritative and indicative of modem practice. It is to be regretted, therefore, that the bulk of the material is dated, and in many cases extremely antiquated.

To the keen enthusiast the opening chapters describing the early history of model aviation in this country are interesting, but the newcomer to aeromodelling, noting the words "First published 1949" on the flyleaf, will be badly misled into thinking that model aeronautical development in this country came to an abrupt halt around the 1930's.

One is left with the impression that the reader of this book who "graduates through the hobby of model aircraft to a career in aviation" will probably initiate his vocation on a B.E.2C.

Frankly, rather a disappointing effort from such a distinguished author.

(C.S.R.)

Modern Boy published F.J.'s paper aeroplane details for cutting out and assembling dated 1929. Alex Imrie in *Aeromodeller* repeated the drawing in 1989 using drawings by Norman Peacock, as a vintage F.J. design. An article "The Golden Jubilee of Aeromodelling" by A.F. Houlberg, M.B.E. (*Aeromodeller*, March 1959) recalled the history of model aviation in the U.K. including F.J. Camm's contributions – he had proposed the name of the Society of Model Aeronautical Engineers which replaced the London Aero Models Association (L.A.M.A.) which F.J. disliked. This important history indicates the famous patrons and council members among which F.J. takes a place.

F.J. adopted the formula originated by Mr E.W. Twining, the English model aeroplane pioneer, e.g. 1-1-P 2 which signifies one leading surface, one main supporting surface, and two pusher screws. This describes a "canard" type – a tractor type would have "P" first.

He also inserted historical notes such as the introduction of elastic motive power by the Frenchman Penaud. One of F.J.'s first models to be included in *Everyday Science* was a simple canard monoplane 1-1-P2.

In addition to Henry Greenly, his contacts included Bassett-Lowkes, the high class model makers of Oxford Street and Northampton.

Several aeromodel designs were included in *Practical Mechanics* Journal after 1933. None appear in his *Practical Mechanics Handbook* (George Newnes, 1938). This is a reference book for the mechanical trades including tables. About 33 pages about "Aeronautical Engineering" were included in his comprehensive volume *Newnes Engineers Reference Book* (many editions after 1946).

One design that seems to be repeated (as in *Hobbies*) is his "Twin Screw Racing Monoplane" which he describes as "An excellent long distance flyer, cheap to make and simple to fly". A canard design, the six pages of instructions stated that "any boy of mechanical ability could make it in a few hours". (Gamages listed a similar model for 25 shillings) (£1.25p). Perhaps this is the design which F.J. flew in a W.M.A.C. competition in August 1914 when it flew out of sight and was lost!

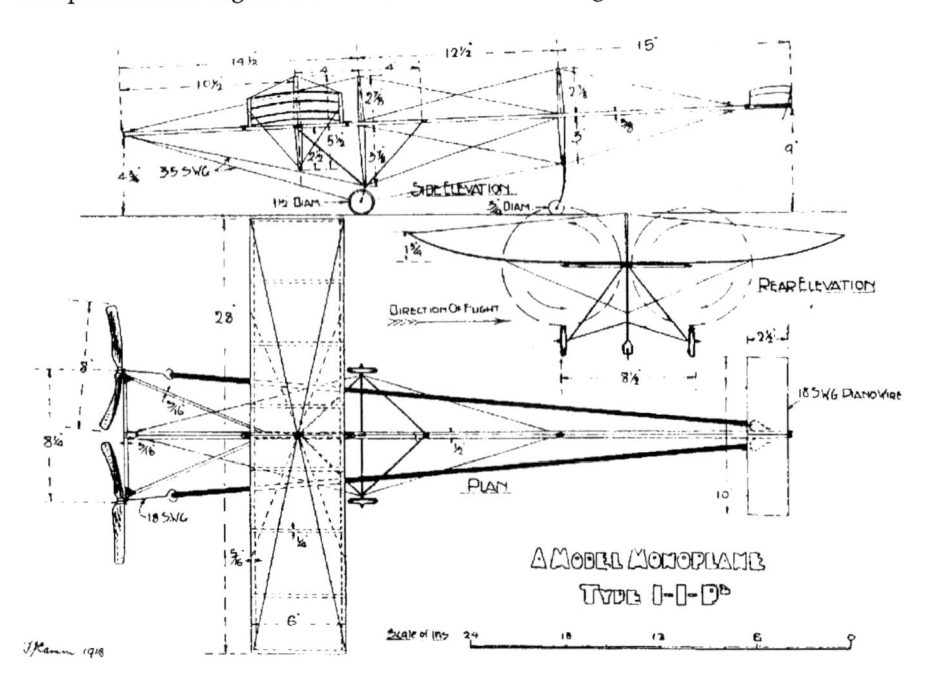

A Model Monoplane Type 1-1-P2

The "Cambro" Cycle Car, of 1919

In 1919, the year of F.J.'s marriage and move to Grove Road, he built a three wheel cycle car with George Camm's help. It was built in the shed behind 10 Alma Road, one object being to enable him to visit Sydney and his wife at Byfleet, sometimes with George perched precariously on the back. Registration number XD3663 was duly licensed – it is not known if he took out third party or other insurance. With a two horsepower twin cylinder air cooled engine, no clutch, no gears (and some say, no brakes) it was started "with two pushes on the pedal". A maximum speed of 47 miles an hour was claimed, and enough power to climb hills of a gradient of one in ten. Test runs to Brighton from London were "made in two and a half hours, at an average speed of 20 miles an hour". The car moved off as soon as the engine was started. Sprung "like an aeroplane" F.J. claimed that the *Cambro* could travel faster on bad roads than a motor cycle, with lower first cost, upkeep and running costs. Later these cars were manufactured by The Central Aircraft Company of Kilburn, N.W.6 and offered for sale at 79 guineas – just under £83.

The original had to be removed from his father's garden shed after removing its side, then lifted over the wall into the adjacent Gas Manager's garden – with Mr Abbott's permission.

The specification was spartan. The engine developed two horsepower from twin opposed cylinders, with a single lever carburettor. The magneto was contained in the flywheel, and the transmission was by chain to the single back wheel. With three cycle type wire wheels, it weighed 150 pounds, had a speed of 20 mph, and did 100 miles per gallon of "petroil" from a half gallon tank. Brakes are not mentioned on the specification leaflet by the Central Aircraft Company of Kilburn. One model survived until about 15 years ago, forgotten in a shed at the British Aero Works at Brooklands. George Camm always claimed that he built the *Cambro* with F.J. and that "Sydney had nothing to do with it".

George Camm said, "…perched on the back, have a chat with Sydney and Hilda at Byfleet and home to Windsor for lunch, we never saw another car or cart and horse on the whole trip. What days!

The Cambro.

Car Comfort with Motor Cycle Simplicity.

Price - 79 Guineas.

MANUFACTURED BY

THE CENTRAL AIRCRAFT COMPANY,

KILBURN, LONDON, N.W.6, ENGLAND.

F.J. Camm and The Design of Model Aeroplanes with Foreword by Frederick Handley Page

From their pre-war school days, the two eldest Camms were keen on model aeroplanes. By 1914 Sydney had written his book *Aeroplane Construction* but the outbreak of war precluded publication until 1919. One illustration in his book was a photograph of one of the biplane gliders built by the Windsor Model Aeroplane Club, the one that had been towed into the air with his younger brother Charles at the "controls" in 1913. With a span of 25 feet, and a weight of 100 pounds, it was greatly admired in Windsor.

In August 1919, F.J. Camm published his own definitive book *The Design of Model Aeroplanes*, which had a Foreword (below) by the famous eminent aviation designer and magnate Frederick Handley Page, who lived nearby at Stanmore. The 172 page book is well illustrated with F.J.'s drawings, and has a photograph of the W.M.A.C. glider. George Camm used to relate that F.J. was unable to find the original photograph he needed of this biplane, so he used the picture torn out of one of Sydney's books – an action that resulted in a dispute devoid of brotherly love at the time. F.J. included complete details of the glider in 20 pages with one or two dozen illustrations. Complete advice was given including the need for a launching hill "for preference 1 in 3", and illustration of the four sections in which it was built – the central cellule (or box), the tail, and two end framed cellules. Spruce timber was used, in the American "Chanute" type design, with interconnected ailerons, a fixed rudder, and wheels 15 inches in diameter (a gift from Maidenhead of salvage from Mr Benton's crash). The frame was covered with unbleached calico, doped with 3:1 varnish and linseed oil. Fittings were made from eighteen gauge steel with weldless steel tube sockets. He used the term "fids" for the brackets and spars junction pins – and explains that the "fid" – a term not in most dictionaries – is the nautical term for the pin supporting the top mast, maintop gallant and royal masts upon their respective caps! One wonders where he learned this information! A pilot's seat is described – and one was certainly made and upholstered by F.J. but some flight photographs appear to show the "pilot" standing up. Piano wire, 18 S.W.G., was used with improvised strainers.

Advice as to attaching towing ropes, selecting take off and landing sites ("preferably soft") and flying weather are included, with the remark that "the average life of a glider is a month". A second edition was required, revised and printed the same year, with the additional information that F.J. was 'Model Editor of *Flight* and Technical Editor of *Everyday Science*'.

The mystery of how F.J. managed to get F. Handley Page to provide the following Foreword remains. He was famous for building the British bombers that rivalled the German Gothas that had ravaged London so that Germany could be bombed successfully. These bombers with their four Rolls Royce engines of 375 h.p. carried five Lewis guns and 7,500 pounds of bombs to drop on Berlin – but only six were complete by the time of the 1918 Armistice. Incidentally, it was F. Handley Page's custom to quote from the scriptures – perhaps F.J. replied as he could have done, recalling his 1910 Champagne Trust prize for Religious Knowledge.

FOREWORD BY MR. HANDLEY PAGE.

THIS book sets forth to explain in non-technical language the theory of artificial flight, through the medium of experiments with model aeroplanes. It requires a very cursory retrospect of the history of flight to realise that the model aeroplane has played a great part in the wresting from nature of the solution to the problems surrounding artificial flight. Model aeroplanes are not toys, but scientific instruments, and it is therefore possible to combine an interesting sport with the fascinating study of the science of aeronautics. The author will be well known as a contributor to the technical press on aeronautical matters, and there can be no doubt that this handbook will be extremely valuable to the student, and is the most authentic work on the subject which has yet appeared. It does not deal merely with the practical side of the subject, but carefully explains the reason why certain causes produce certain effects, and the chapter on " WHY AN AEROPLANE FLIES is explained in verbiage not beyond the ken of the average reader, although it is not written down to him. In the ensuing years aircraft is going to play an important part in the commercial and national interests of all nations, and only those competent in aeronautics can acquire the positions eventually to be had. No more certain way of acquainting oneself with the alpha and omega exists than the making and flying of model aeroplanes. These are within the means of everybody to make, and there is no reason why the subject should not become part of the curriculum of our technical schools and colleges. Mr. Camm's book reveals the touch of the engineer, and is commended both to the student and the man who flies model aeroplanes for sport, as being written in an interesting style, easily understood, with first-rate illustrations.

F. HANDLEY PAGE.

PREFACE

Many text books have been written upon the various branches of Aeronautical Science and Engineering. Almost without exception they deal with the higher mathematical side of the question and, useful as they are to the Aeronautical Engineer, few of them can be said to remove the difficulties encountered in the study of the problem by those who may not possess a knowledge of mathematics.

IT has been my aim in this book to present the reader with as nontechnical a description as is possible of the functions which the various components are called upon to perform. Be building and flying of the various models illustrated and described herein will serve to apply those principles; and in the general manipulation of them I hope the reader may thereby be led to seriously study the absorbing Science of Aeronautics.

In the construction of the full size glider dealt with at the end of the book, it is also possible to obtain a fair ken of piloting, and to experience some of the joys of being in the air.

Having once mastered the fundamental principles of artificial fight, and by study improved his knowledge of mathematical calculation, the text books previously alluded to will then assist the reader to a more concerted study of the subject.

NEVERTHELESS, in the construction of the machines dealt with in this book, I hope the reader may find amusement as well as interest in what, to many people is one of the most fascinating pursuits which Science has given to us.

F. J. CAMM, WINDSOR. August 1919.

Flying the Atlantic project

The W.M.A.C. did not survive the war. There had been financial difficulties and conscription. In 1914 the club lost Sydney to Martinsyde for war work – he took part in the design of a giant monoplane in which Gustav Hamel was to attempt to fly the Atlantic, a feat for which Lord Northcliffe's *Daily Mail* offered in 1914 £10,000 for the first non-stop flight. Gustav Hamel was lost over the Channel, and the war resulted in the project being shelved.

In 1919 four attempts were commenced to build aeroplanes to win the £10,000. All were being built in Newfoundland, where there were no hangars, so work took place in the open. The four were Sopwith, Vickers Vimy, Martinsyde and Handley Page. Sydney was concerned with the Martinsyde attempt, and F.J. was in touch with Frederick Handley Page, so perhaps the Camms could discuss the matter.

The fields of Newfoundland were small and uneven, so take-offs were difficult. The first machine to attempt a flight was the Martinsyde, which crashed on take off.

The next was Henry Hawker who managed to take off the single engined Sopwith on 18th May 1989, but never arrived in the U.K. Many days later it was found that he had made a forced landing in the Atlantic alongside a Danish ship after a flight of 1,400 miles.

In June, Captain John Alcock was the pilot of the Vickers Vimy, a wartime bomber adaptation. Lieutenant Arthur Whitten Brown was navigator, and they just managed to take off from a small hill top field followed by an exhausting 1,890 mile flight ending in an Irish bog.

The Handley Page entry was promptly withdrawn, and diverted towards New York to make demonstration flights. It crashed after a series of engine cooling difficulties, as Sydney related to F.J.

In 1922 F.J. became a founder member of the Society of Model Aeronautical Engineers, previously the Kite and Model Aeroplane Association.

F.J. Camm's The Design of Model Aeroplanes (1919)

F.J.'s first book *The Design of Model Aeroplanes* (1919), 172 pages with Index, contains more illustrations than space allows to be reproduced.

In addition to "Types of Model Aeroplanes", the contents page lists: A simple monoplane; A twin screw monoplane. (Sometimes this appears to be entitled "A long distance monoplane" such as F.J. described and illustrated in *Models, Railways and Locomotives*, June 1918 type 1-1-P2) referred to above); A twin screw biplane; a tractor monoplane; A tractor biplane; A hydro monoplane; A compressed air model; as well as a man carrying glider. He details the making of the various component parts of the models.

I have selected the first model "A simple monoplane", and "A tractor biplane". F.J. introduces the latter stating that "it secured the second highest marks for design and construction in the 1914 Aero Show competitions at Hendon, and took fifth place in the flying tests – a good result as it was competing against monoplanes …"

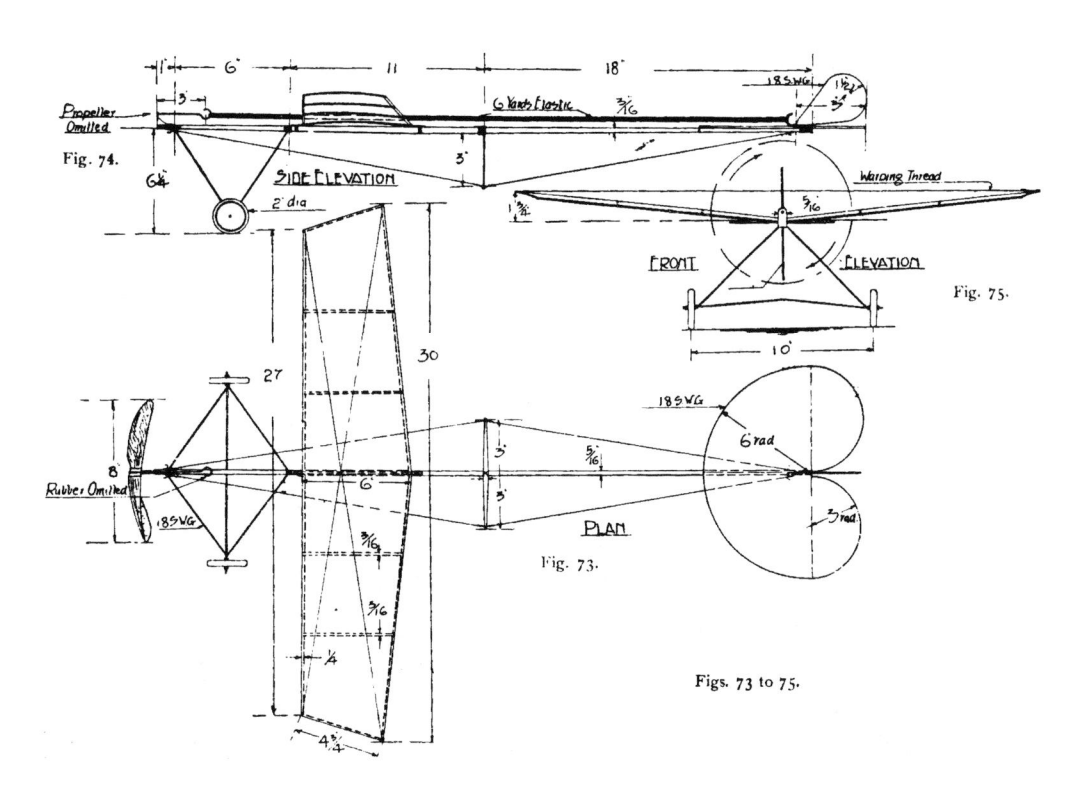

Figs. 73 to 75.

A Tractor Monoplane

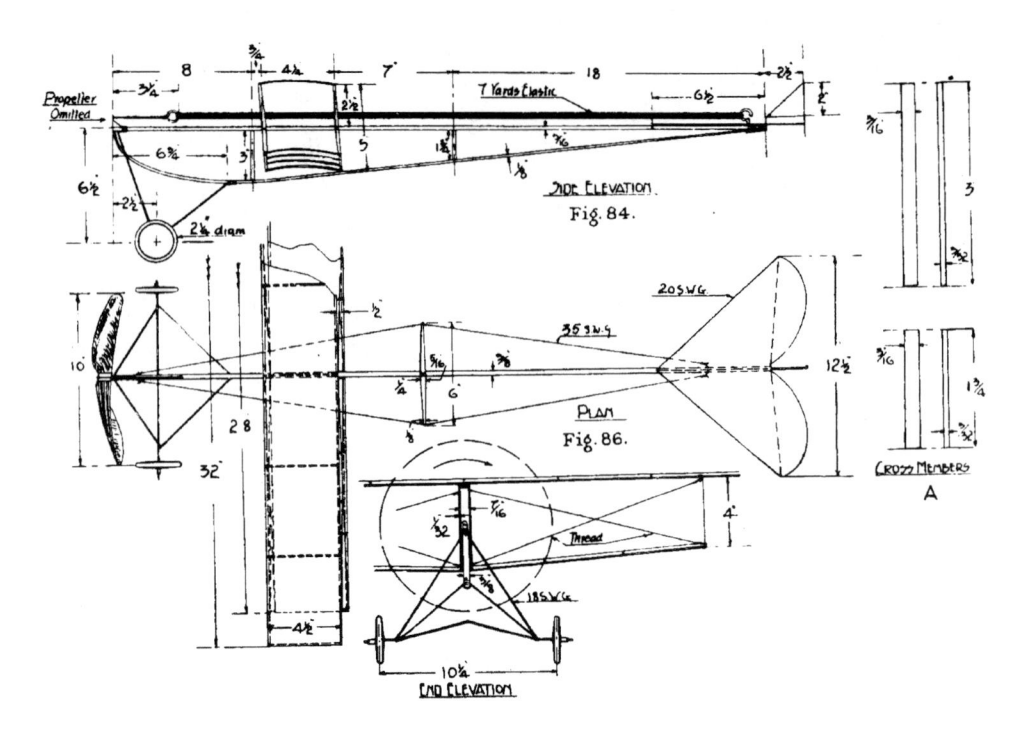

A Tractor Biplane

How did the Camm pilots learn to fly the W.M.A.C. gliders?

Perhaps they had learned about the "Dynamic resistance of a plane". By 1909 authors such as Robert W.A. Brewer, A.M.I.C.E., M.I. Mec.E. etc, in his *The Art of Aviation* had used Newton's theory and formulae such as Langley's, Joessel and Aranzini's to arrive at the view that for conditions of stability the centre of gravity and the centre of pressure from the planes should coincide. (In actual flight the centre of gravity should be slightly ahead of the centre of pressure.)

In practice, either the centre of pressure should be moved by adjusting the planes, or the centre of gravity by shifting the body or legs in imitation of a bird. The Wrights decided that the former was better, but Sydney Camm is said by George Camm to have instructed his pilots not to touch the "controls", but to move their weight. In *Building a Glider* F.J. states that "control is by means of Bowden cable connected to a rocking bar actuated by the joystick" without further comment. To this end the pilots stood at first, but a seat – provided by F.J. – was available. F.J. specified that "the pilot's seat is constructed of three-ply and aluminium upholstered lightly with pegamoid. It is adjustable in a fore and aft direction, so that the c.p. (centre of pressure) and c.g. (centre of gravity) may be made to coincide".

At least two crashes tended to throw some doubt on the matter, but a third tractor biplane was completed except for the covering of the wings when the outbreak of war in 1914 brought this project to an end and Sydney left Windsor to join Martinsyde's – a firm started by H.P. Martin and G.H. Handasyde.

Engines being underpowered tended to be run at full load, and lubrication, over heating and metal failures were common. One of the conditions for the tests of engines for the £1,000 Patrick Y. Alexander prize in 1909 was that the engines must be run for a period of one hour in either direction at an inclination of 15 degrees. Such tests were beyond the resources of the Camms with the engine they had acquired for £25 from the Irish aviatrix, Miss Bland. This was an air cooled 2 cylinder 20 b.h.p. (alleged) Cowley originally owed by A.V. Roe – who found it underpowered. It was thought that one horse power was required for every 34 pounds weight of the machine when loaded. The glider weight without the engine was 100 pounds.

In September 1922 Sydney Camm flew as Raynham's mechanic in a Martinsyde F-6 in the first King's Cup Air Race circuit of Britain. In *Everyday Science*, October 1922, F.J. wrote:

F.P. Raynham and the first King's Cup Air Race

"All who know Raynham will express regret at his having lost the race; the margin however, was so narrow that, virtually his performance was as good as the winners. The writer's brother accompanied Raynham on this flight, and some of the photos taken from the air during the race will probably be published in this section next month".

Sydney's daughter, Mrs Phyllis Dixon flew to San Diego with Dr Fozard in October 1984 for the investiture of her father as the seventh Britisher to be so honoured in the International Hall of Fame. In her response to the award she mentioned that it had been her second ever flight, and her first jet flight, and that her father would never have been persuaded to fly 7,000 miles aboard a jet liner to get to San Diego!

I have not found one record of F.J. flying, but in 1934 he claimed to have flown a glider.

F.J. The Glider Pilot

In an article entitled "Learning to Glide", in *Practical Mechanics* November 1934 (pages 50/51) F.J. wrote "There is a peculiar fascination in gliding. I can write with first hand knowledge of it for, before the war, I designed, built and flew several full-sized gliders, one of which is illustrated below".

He went on to describe "the remarkable 'silence' when, seated in a glider, you attain a height of a few thousand feet". The claim *"and flew"* appears apocryphal.

This glider was not priced, but F.J. went on to state: "The parts will not cost more than £3 or £4, and the work is well within the ability of any amateur capable of making a few simple metal fittings and who is reasonably skilled in the use of woodworking tools" ...

The club members continued to make models, which F.J. reported to *Flight*, but their numbers dwindled as some – including Charles Camm – joined the forces.

F.J. flew models for the Castle gunners to practise aiming during the 1914-18 war. The boys used to cycle to watch pre-war displays at Hendon and Brooklands. Sydney was allowed to inspect captured enemy aircraft at the Agricultural Hall, Islington. He noted the sloped back wings of the Stahlaube and Rampler Taube monoplanes – a feature that F.J. seems to have copied, also the Albatross biplanes.

In addition to the W.M.A.C. shed in Arthur Road, F.J. had a retreat from the crowded little house at 10 Alma Road in his father's carpentry shed behind the house.

Here the engine bought in 1913 was brought and tested. Later F.J.'s cycle experiments were made, including the Cambro cycle car he built with George Camm's help in 1919, to visit Sydney and his wife – with George perched precariously on the back. Here F.J. worked on the automatic cycle tyre pump which he patented. It inflated the tyre when the cycle was being ridden along – a feature he demonstrated years later during a BBC T.V. programme.

With no side entry to the terrace house, access was not easy – the Cambro had to be lifted over the wall into the Gas Manager's garden, with Mr Abbott's permission. F.J. experimented with propeller design for his models. In 1922 he was appointed a judge for the Society of Model Aero Engineers Propeller Competition – a society some of whose members were not always in agreement with F.J.

The glider – or aeroplane – was said by F.J. to have been broken up in 1919, and the engine was cherished by George Camm for many years until it was lent to the Windsor Collection, then part of a display in Windsor Guildhall. It is now in store in the Borough Depot where the Royal Windsor Collection has been kept since the Guildhall display was closed in 1982. Years later Lilian Bland – who had married a cousin, and ranched in America for many years – returned to this country. She telephoned George Camm to ask "What happened to my engine?"

Model Flying Machines designed by F.J.

The following is F.J.'s contribution to a Ward, Lock & Co. Ltd publication *The Handy Boy's Book* published in the 1920s.

MODEL FLYING MACHINES
SINGLE AND TWIN-SCREW MONOPLANES THAT ANY
BOY CAN MAKE
BY F. J. CAMM

A PAIR of pliers, a small chisel and a hammer, one very fine bradawl and an ordinary fretwork plane, comprise all the tools required.

Some of the materials, however, can be bought so cheaply that it will hardly be worth while to make them. I refer chiefly to the wood for the mainplanes and propellers, and also the wooden frame, or fuselage, members.

A SIMPLE SINGLE-SCREW MONOPLANE

A Single Screw Monoplane

A glance at the drawings will convey the form and general arrangement of this model. It is a single-screw monoplane, and it flies with the propeller behind, not leading, as in most of the fullsize machines. In other words it is a "pusher," not a " tractor." The screw is placed in the rear because it is much simpler to fly the machine thus, and not nearly so much adjustment is necessary.

The first thing to do is to plane the wood for the frame, or body, to the sizes shown on the drawing. Great care must be exercised to ensure that both pieces are of exactly the same length and section, so that they are of the same weight. It is a good plan to weigh each member separately, gradually planing a shaving or so off the heavier until they are equal in weight. The pieces can be finished up smoothly with fine No. 00 sandpaper. It will be noticed that the frame members taper slightly off towards each end. This is to prevent the completed frame from buckling or twisting under the stress of the elastic motor.

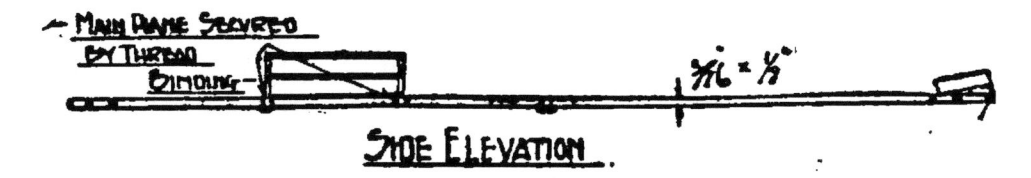

A narrow strip of brass will next be required to form the bearing, as sketched. It should be about one thirty-second of an inch in thickness, the two lugs which engage the frame members being so bent that they follow the contour, or curve, of the bowed frame. A one-sixteenth hole must be drilled in the centre for the spindle of the propeller to pass through, as will be seen from the plan view.

The bearing is to be tightly bound to the members with black threecord carpet thread, the thread being afterwards smeared with weak glue to secure it. It should be lashed after the manner of the binding on a cricket bat and the ends pulled through out of sight.

Now bend to the shape shown in the sketch the hook which passes through the nose of the machine, and to which the other end of the elastic skein is attached. It will be clear from the sketch that its end is bent round flush to the frame member, and is tightly lashed and glued into position. Before the two frame members can be bound, however, they must be cut off to an angle as shown in the sketch.

We now have the bearing and the hook attached; it only remains to bow the frame to complete it. This is effected by fixing a cross member, also shown in perspective detail, across the frame and firmly securing it by pins, glue, and binding.

The elevator is formed from either piano or tinned iron wire—the former for preference, since it is more durable and not nearly so likely to buckle should it receive a knock during flying. It is made in one piece, as a glance at the elevator plan will show. The centre rib continues over the leading edge, being bent downwards and backward, as shown in the sketch of the centre rib of the elevator. This projecting spoke provides the means of securing the elevator to the frame. It is passed through a hole drilled in the nose of the frame so that the spoke is a nice fit within it; the spoke being bent back at an angle, causes the trailing edge of the elevator to bind on to the spar. No further security will be found necessary, as the elevator will remain quite rigidly in place during flying, although, should the model strike a tree, wall or other object, it will swivel round and so will not be damaged. The joint in it (which, it must be noticed, is located at the centre of the back, or trailing, edge) must be bound with fine florists tinned wire and lightly soldered. It will also, of course, require to be soldered where the centre rib passes over the front, or leading edge and continues downward to form the adjusting spoke. Finally, carefully true it up with the pliers so that it lies quite flat.

So much for the elevator; we can now turn to the main plane. This is built up of thin strips of wood pinned and glued together as shown in detail. The best method to adopt for its construction is to leave both spars and ribs a trifle longer (say half an inch) than necessary, so that they do not become split during the pinning operation. Mark ribs and spars off to correct lengths and pin them together, placing the ribs on the top of the spars, smearing glue with a camel-hair brush between the joint, and driving the pins right through into the bench.

The plane should be left thus secured until the glue has thoroughly set, when it may be prized up with the blade of a pocket-knife, the pins bent over or " clinched " into the spars, by tapping them back with a small hammer (the wing being supported on an iron block during this operation), and the ribs then trimmed off flush with the spars. Carefully remove with fine sandpaper any sharp edges which might tear through the fabric, and the wing frame is complete.

It will be the better plan, I think, to complete all the components before covering the two planes, so we may proceed to the final and, be it said, the most important part of the machine, the propeller. This is to be cut from very thin wood (birch for preference), of the shape and dimensions shown, and bent as explained below to the shape indicated in the plan view of the model. Around the centre of the blank a tin strap is to be soldered, and on to this, in turn, the shaft is also soldered. It must be clearly understood that the shaft passes over the centre of the blank, and thus must be soldered to both sides of it. Before forming the hook;, a short length of brass tubing must be slipped on the shaft to act as a distance bush to allow the propeller to clear the frame when it is revolving. Now hold the blades in a jet of steam and gently twist along the dotted bending lines shown in the drawing until, under the warping effect of the steam, it remains where twisted. One blade only must be operated on at a time, and each must be bent to exactly the same degree. Too much care cannot be expended on the making of the propeller, for on its efficient working the whole success of the machine depends.

Readers who prefer to buy a propeller can do so from any of the London model-dealers for a shilling or so, although it is obviously more interesting for the reader to prepare his own. Take note that the screw is made to revolve in the direction of the arrows in the end elevation of the model. When satisfied that the propeller is quite true, it can be sand papered and polished with a couple of coats of good coach varnish, and then left to dry.

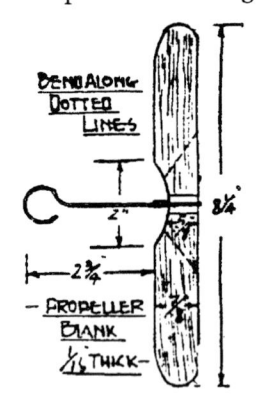

Reverting now to the question of covering, nothing better or lighter can be used than yellow Jap silk, which, when varnished, is of a rather pleasing golden hue; as only half a yard will suffice the cost of fabric will not be great The edges of the fabric are to be glued along the spars, so as to present a neat top appearance. First, cut the fabric out to size, allowing sufficient to pull under the spars, and then glue it to the under surface of either of the two end ribs and leave to dry. When set, pull the fabric tautly over the frame so that the latter bends up slightly as shown in the end view, and glue along under the second end rib. The bowing up of the frame, it will be noticed, has a tendency to prevent- this end from sticking, so drawing pins must be inserted, being pressed partially home into the rib until the glue has set. Finally, stretch the fabric over the leading and trailing edges of the plane, using drawing pins as before, and taking care that all wrinkles in the fabric are effaced. All rough edges should be cut away with the scissors. In order that the main plane may maintain its upward curve as shown in the end view it is to be diagonally braced with carpet thread.

With regard to the elevator, it will be found expedient to sew the fabric to this, first pinning it tautly into place and then securing it with an over and over stitch.

END ELEVATION

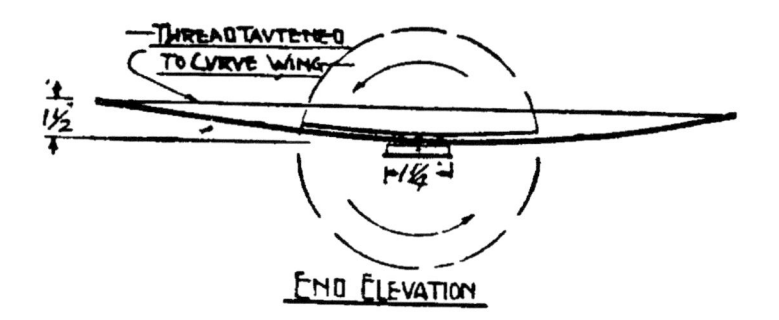

We now arrive at the proofing stage. I cannot lay too much stress upon the importance of making the covering thoroughly impervious to air, as that is where so many beginners go astray. The fabric must be quite airtight. The best proofing to use is good varnish, slightly diluted with turps to dry it more quickly. This mixture should be thinly and evenly applied with a flat brush, one or more coats being given according to the appearance of the fabric after the first. The planes must be viewed after proofing (or " doping ") for pores, and it is upon the presence or otherwise of those pores that the necessity for a second coat depends.

When the wing is thoroughly dry it may be bound to the frame (which should previously have been varnished), as shown in the side elevation. As will be obvious, the binding passes over the spars of the wing and round the frame members, and thus secures it.

Now place the elevator in position, with its front edge about an eighth of an inch off the frame, as shown in the sketch of the centre rib (the trailing edge, of course, being down on the frame), pass the propeller spindle through the bearing, and attach the skein of rubber to the hooks By the way, make quite sure that the correct elastic is procured, that is three-sixteenths by one thirty-second of an inch. The hooks can also be conveniently covered with cycle-valve tubing to prevent them from cutting through the rubber. All joins or breakages in the latter must be repaired with thread, the elastic to be stretched while being bound with it.

Before we can actually fly the machine we shall require some rubber lubricant. This is used to prevent the strands from adhering to one another, and also to enable more turns to be given to the skein, which means, of course, more power. The ingredients are soft soap and glycerine in the proportion 6: I, well boiled together and allowed to cool. When smeared upon the strands of rubber this solution has the desired effect of rendering them slippery.

And now with regard to the actual flying of the machine.

In the first place the model must be glided, to adjust its balance. Hold it aloft just above the head, the left hand supporting the front and the right grasping the propeller. Impart a gentle forward thrust to the model with the right hand, at the same time releasing the left. As the right arm comes forward, release the machine, and if it is correctly balanced it should glide to earth at a very slight angle. Assuming, however, that it has a tendency to dive, then the mainplane must be moved forward. If, on the other hand, it has a tendency to rise, the mainplane must be moved to the rear. This adjustment, of course, necessitates the removal of the binding holding the mainplane to the frame. Hence I would suggest that it be only temporarily lashed in the first instance to facilitate its being quickly adjusted on the field, Unless the tendency to dive or ascend is abnormal, the main plane must not be moved more than three thirty- seconds of an inch, in either direction, at a time.

Having by this means obtained an even glide, the model can be tested in actual flight by giving the propeller from 100 to 150 turns in the correct direction, which must be such that the screw, when unwinding, drives a volume of air from the rear end of the machine. There is a very erroneous idea prevalent among beginners that a propeller may be wound in either direction. Such is not the case, as the reader will see if he endeavours to fly the machine with the screw wound the wrong way round.

To launch the model grasp the screw in the right hand and support the nose with the left, as if about to glide the model. Then thrust it forward with the right, at the same time releasing the left; and when the right has travelled sufficiently far forward that, too, may be released. If all is in order, the model should rise and fly steadily.

Should it tend to dive slightly, or to " stall " (rise at too steep an angle), then similar adjustments as were made when gliding are required. Once the most favourable position for the wing is found it can be permanently bound there in the manner already described, and any small adjustments necessary afterwards can be effected by altering the angle of the elevator by pushing the spoke passing through the frame upward to increase the elevation or downward to lessen it.

The maximum number of turns the elastic will stand is 350, and this number should be gradually worked up to, and not applied until you are quite certain that the model is correctly adjusted.

Keep the bearing well vaselined, lubricating the rubber every third or fourth flight; and if the model has been made according to these instructions, circular flights of from 150 to 200 yards should be easily obtained.

Should the propeller have a tendency to chatter during revolution the propeller shaft must be adjusted until it revolves truly.

A TWIN-SCREW MONOPLANE

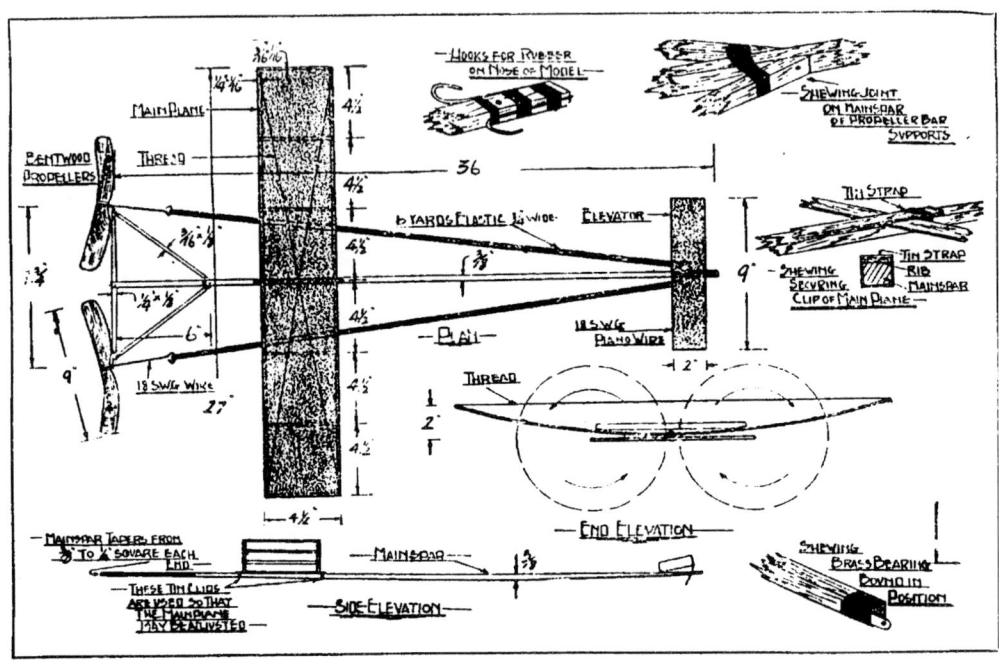

Twin-Screw Monoplane

A Twin Screw Monoplane

The twin-screw monoplane illustrated is just a little more difficult than the machine described in the preceding pages. It will carry the reader a little beyond the constructional ability required for that machine, but it should afford him an opportunity of applying the experience gained thereby. This machine, it will be observed, possesses twin screws, revolving in opposite directions. These are fitted in order to obtain as straight a flight as possible. Those who have built and flown the model first described will have noticed that it had a tendency to fly in a circle, in an opposite direction to that in which the screw revolves. This is, of course, a difficulty that can be got over in many other ways, but it follows that if we use twin propellers revolving in opposite directions each will balance the twisting effect of the other. Whatever other methods we may employ, this is the most mechanical.

This design is one that is, in a more elaborate form, much in favour with some of our crack aeromodellists. In fact, I believe it has figured more in open competitions than any other. This is not surprising, for from the point of view of those who fly models for sport (and an excellent form of sport, too), better flying results could hardly be desired. The minimum distance this model should fly is 300 yards at an altitude of forty to sixty feet.

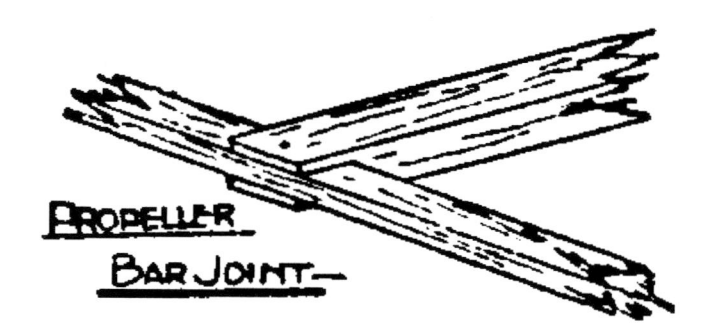

PROPELLER BAR JOINT

The plan view will show the principal dimensions and the general arrangement. The twin screws are driven by two skeins of elastic, disposed diagonally in relation to the mainspar. It will be seen that the frame is of the T pattern, so called because of its resemblance to that letter. The two propeller bearings are carried on a bar, which is supported by two diagonal struts.

It will be best to construct the frame first. Carefully taper the mainspar as shown in the drawing, and then with a narrow chisel or fretsaw cut a slot in one end to receive the propeller-bar, as sketched in detail. Make the propeller-bar a tight fit within the slot, and then pin and glue it into place. A sketch is also included of the joint of the propeller-bar supports, which clearly indicates that it is pinned and bound into place. All binding should be saturated with weak glue so that it remains secure. It is essential that the propeller-bar support joint should be a sound one, because it has to withstand the tension of two skeins of rubber, and this is considerable.

To each end of the propeller-bar a small brass bearing is attached (made from similar brass to that used on the single-screw model) by tight lashing and glueing.

Twin hooks are fitted to the front of the frame as shown. The hole for the elevator adjusting spoke (shown also in the drawing) must not be drilled until after the hooks are bound in, as there is less likelihood of the spar splitting during the insertion of the drill. In this machine, it will be

RIB JOINT

seen, a different method of securing the mainplane to the spar is employed. The centre rib continues over the edges of the spar, and is clipped to the latter by means of tin clips or sockets. This permits of the wing being readily adjusted or removed, and at the same time provides a rigid wing security. I have shown the detail in perspective, as well as in section, so that it shall be quite clear. The tin strap should be tightly pulled round the rib and spar before it is soldered up, to ensure that the plane will not be loose within it.

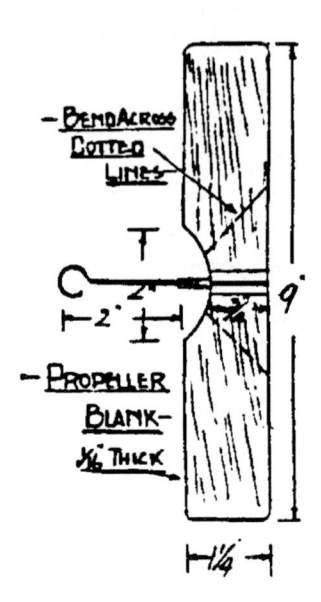

The mainplane and elevator are made in a similar manner to those used for the first machine, the ribs and spars being left longer than necessary to be trimmed off flush when the glue has set. In covering the mainplane use great care to ensure that the plane does not become warped owing to the fabric being pulled too taut. Varnish and turps are again to be used to proof the wing, two coats being given if necessary. When the plane and the elevator are fixed it is necessary to sight along them to see that they are in line with one another. A view of the end elevation will reveal clearly what is meant.

The mainplane is to be diagonally braced to impart the upward curve; the ends of the bracing threads are passed through small holes drilled through the spar, just inside the end ribs, and then knotted. Carpet thread or fine Jap gut is suitable for the purpose. If the reader has prepared his own wood, the bracing of the mainplane will at once reveal any thin spots in the spars, by showing a broken curve. ' It is most important that the wood should be planed of uniform thickness.

The bending of the propellers will require special attention because they are of opposite pitch, which means that we have four blades to bend at the same angle and at the same position in relation to the spindle. If, however, the reader keeps before him the plan view of the screws during bending I do not think he can go wrong. As with the previous machine, bend along the dotted lines, finishing one blade at a time, and do not try to twist two at the same time. After bending they must be thoroughly dried in front of the fire to draw out all moisture from the grain.

In flying the model remember that the propellers must be wound in opposite directions, and that each must be wound exactly the same number of times. Launch the machine with the right hand grasping both propellers, the left supporting the front of the machine, and be sure to launch on an even keel. For ease in launching it will be found best to place the screws to revolve outwardly, that is, the righthand screw should be placed on the right-hand bearing (facing the line of flight), and the left-hand propeller on the left-hand bearing. Finally, keep the bearings well vaselined and the rubber lubricated, and apply the same methods of adjustment as advocated for the single-screw monoplane.

F.J. Camm and the Model Engineer exhibition of 1935

The following is an extract from the *Practical Mechanics* published November 1935: It is one of the most sophisticated models, and the blue prints of F.J. Camm's 'Petrol Driven Monoplane' were very popular.

A Petrol-driven Model Monoplane

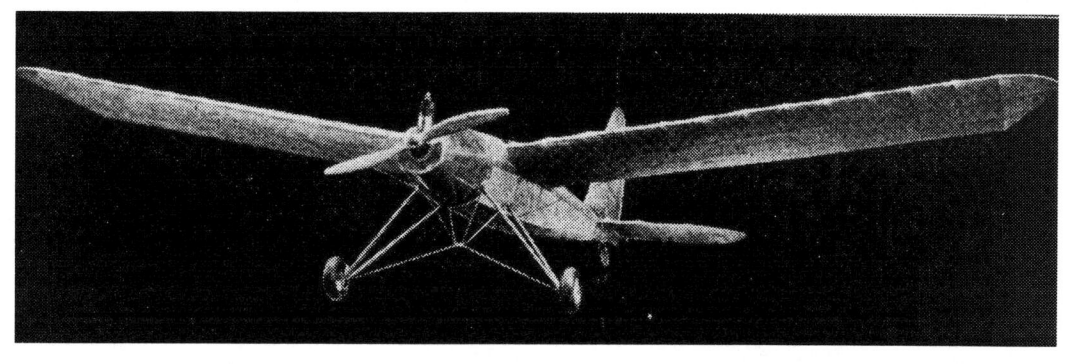

The completed model—the first concerning which detailed designs and full-size blueprints have been published.

Final Details of this Fine Flying Model
By F. J. Camm.

AS mentioned last month, I loaned the model shown in the photograph above to the Model Engineer Exhibition, and I have not had an opportunity of photographing the model in flight since then. It is difficult to launch a petrol-driven model and then to endeavour to pick hold of a camera and photograph it. I have made arrangements, however, for the services of a photographer on the next fine week-end.

The Ignition Circuit

I HAVE received dozens of letters from readers who are building it, and one or two of them have asked for details of the ignition circuit. This I have pleasure in giving this month in the diagram on page 110. It will be seen that one lead from the coil goes to the sparking plug, one primary lead being connected to one lead of a fixed condenser, and then earthed to any convenient point on the engine cradle. The other side of the condenser passes to the insulated contact breaker and the two leads to the battery and switch are led off as shown. This arrangement is far better than that normally adopted where the accumulator is left in circuit, and in parallel with the dry cell when the switch is thrown over. In my arrangement the accumulator is cut out and the dry cell cut in instantaneously, since the switch is of the quick make-and-break type. I would repeat that the full-size blueprints listed on this page will facilitate construction. The supply is limited, and is running short. The positions of the wings shown on the blue prints are very approximately correct, and only a slight movement of the dry cell is necessary in order to make the centre of gravity coincide with the centre of pressure. I have found that the thrust line is ideal, although in some cases it may be desirable to bend the tail flaps up to improve longitudinal stability. A negative angle on the whole tail also improves stability, and this can be arranged by adjusting the tube fixed to the rear of the tail before soldering it.

Inverted Engines

A LOT of readers have written to me asking whether it would be advisable to invert the engine, as is sometimes done. My answer to this is an emphatic No! It serves no purpose whatever to do so, and merely provides one of the humorous aspects of model aeroplaning. It places the cylinder in its most vulnerable position, and it enables oil to drain down on to the plug, thus giving rise to misfiring and other ignition troubles. It does not lower the centre of gravity of the machine at all, and I have failed to discover any sound reason for placing the engine in any other than the correct position. Another disadvantage is that you will put yourself to a considerable amount of trouble inverting the carburetter and tank arrangements.

The size of the model can be estimated from this photograph.

> **BLUEPRINTS OF F. J. CAMM'S PETROL-DRIVEN MODEL MONOPLANE**
>
> The following full-size blueprints are now ready and may be obtained, at the prices mentioned, from the publishers: George Newnes Ltd., 8–11 Southampton Street, Strand, London, W.C.2:
>
> **Sheet 1, price 1s.**
> This blueprint gives the shape of each bulkhead, the engine cradle, and the stiffeners.
>
> **Sheet 2, price 1s.**
> Shows the rudder and tail full-size with methods of fixing.
>
> **Sheet 3, price 4s.**
> Shows the fuselage full-size in side elevation and plan, the holding-down strap for coil, chassis construction, rear wheel and suspension, switch and ignition circuit, wing fixings and method of bracing.
>
> **Sheet 4, price 1s. 6d.**
> Full-size plan of the mainplane, full-size rib section and wing couplings.
>
> **Sheet 5, price 6d.**
> Full-size plan of engine adapter for the Atom Minor, Hallam, Grayspee, Andrich, and Economic engines.

F.J. Camm the Cyclist and the "Werner" model

The elder Camm boys managed to acquire bicycles. These were expensive – the higher grades cost £18 new, but machines were available from about £7. This took a lot of saving from an apprentice's wage of a shilling a week for each year of service. The machines provided transport to cyclists' meetings, and to model aeroplane club meetings, as well as "real" aeroplane displays, such as the big machines that Sydney was interested in at Brooklands and Farnborough.

F.J. devised and eventually patented an automatic cycle pump worked by the revolving cycle wheels. Slow punctures were the bane of cyclists from the sharp flints of untarred roads.

He later made a one eighth scale model of the *Werner* light motor cycle, from a machine he examined at the Science Museum. This has a single cylinder engine on the handlebars which powered the front wheel by a belt drive. His model won the first prize at the 1954 Auto Cycle Union Moto Cycle competition in the Pioneer class.

The stock of patent pumps and the Werner model eventually reached his brother George after F.J.'s death, and disappeared (after George died in 1987) with other F.J. models, as reported later.

F.J. Camm's prize winning model of the 1897 Werner. The competition was organised by the Auto-Cycle Union

F.J.'s interests included cycle road racing, and cycle records. He published the national and local records for timed rides between local "Derbys" as well as the prestigious Lands End to John O'Groats rides, in his *Every Cyclists Handbook*. After this had been out of print for several years, he updated the information in his *Every Cyclists Pocket Book*. The latter included advice on cycling abroad and material that he said would "meet the needs of the racing cyclist, the tourist cyclist, and the mechanic, including cycling law, road lighting, camping and clothing". He reminded cyclists that rear lights became compulsory on cycles after February 1946.

Women's records had not been included until F.J. listed these retrospectively from 1935. The holds of records "since the unpaced era began" were included from 1898.

He was opposed to cycle paths, and derided what he termed the "eternal parrot cry" for cycle paths on every new road, and accepted the claim that these paths took up an extra five and a half acres for every mile of new road.

In 1950 he wrote "For the greater part of a long business career I cycled to and from my job", adding that "this involved two and a half miles four times a day for six years", without explanation as to where or when. Subsequently he chafed at the delays due to queuing and elbowing before getting a place on a public service vehicle.

He once strongly supported the British League of Racing Cyclists – who advocated massed start road racing in opposition to the National Cyclists' Union who "went behind the scenes to get it suppressed". The Ministry and Home Office announced that massed start racing was undesirable and issued veiled threats of dire penalties (c. 1950?).

F.J. applauded the publicity for road racing. As Editor of *The Cyclist* he was concerned with the Macmillan Centenary Pilgrimage into Wales in 1939 to honour the Scots builder in 1839 of the first velocipede bicycles. (See Titbits, 22nd April 1939 – '100 years on two wheels'). Eventually paper rationing and shortages resulted in his editorship of *The Cyclist* having to be incorporated with *Practical Mechanics*. One item in 1955 informed readers that cyclists could now take their machines to France for as little extra as two shillings and sixpence (12^1/$_2$p) via Silver City Airways from Lydd (Ferryfield) to Calais/Le Touquet. The extra to Ostend was five shillings (25p).

In 1944 the Windsor Express reported that F.J. and Sydney had patented (?) a super bicycle both rust proof and thief proof, incorporating improvements which had been war time secrets!

(I found that Mr Lionel Joseph of the CTC Cyclists Touring Club, Godalming is working on the old material, pre computer, as are others "because of the forthcoming centenary" and therefore I did not wish to duplicate research).

His earliest known motor cycling interests are recorded in the *Motor Cyclists' Pocket Book* which he wrote as 'Waysider' for Sir Isaac Pitman while at Windsor in 1923.

The Propeller competition of 1922

In 1922 F.J. was appointed one of two judges for a propeller competition held under the auspices of the Society of Model Aero Engineers.

F.J. subsequently published the results:

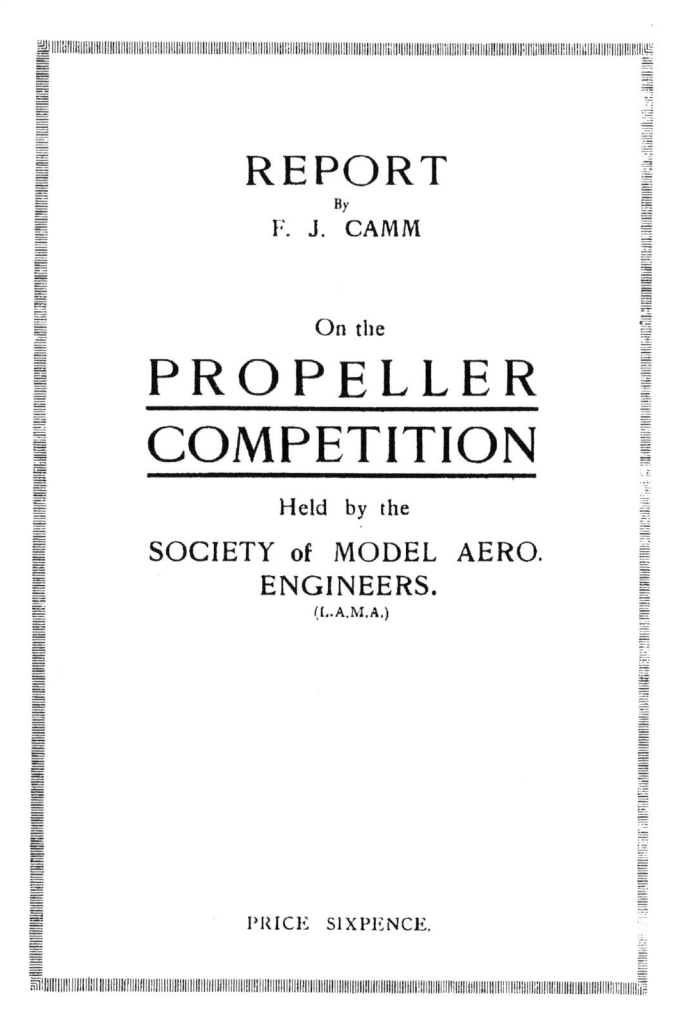

REPORT
By
F. J. CAMM

On the

PROPELLER
COMPETITION

Held by the
SOCIETY of MODEL AERO.
ENGINEERS.
(L.A.M.A.)

PRICE SIXPENCE.

RESULTS OF PROPELLER COMPETITION

By F. J. Camm.

An interesting propeller competition was held under the auspices of the Society of Model Aero. Engineers on Saturday, March 25, 1922, at 6 p.m., in the club-room, 20, Great Windmill Street, Piccadilly Circus. The donor of the prizes was H. J. Best, Esq. The first prize was £1 5s., and there were also second and third prizes. The judges were Mr. F. J. Camm and Mr. W. E. Evans, and the competition was governed by the following rules:—

1. The competition is open to all.

2. Entrance free to members and graduate members. Entrance fee, 1s., for non-members.

3. Propellers are to be designed and constructed entirely by competitors.

4. One propeller only may be entered by each competitor, and two-bladed propellers only are allowed.

5. Diameter, 12 in.; pitch 18 in. Size of hole at boss, $\frac{1}{8}$ in.; maximum weight, 1 oz.; minimum weight, $\frac{1}{2}$ oz.

6. The pitch angle, 35 deg. 35 mins., will be tested at 4 in. from tip of blade, and the pitch angle, 26 deg. 30 mins., at $\frac{1}{4}$ in. from tip of blade.

7. The actual thrust will be taken in conjunction with duration of run, thereby measuring horse-power.

8. Competitors must mark the number of their entry form plainly on their propeller, no other markings being allowed.

As this competition is the first of its kind held, and as the results obtained are extremely valuable, it is here dealt with in full. There were fifteen entries, the majority of the screws being well finished. All were carved from the solid block save one, which was laminated.

Rejections.—Each screw was tested first for weight and then for pitch angles; every possible allowance was made for screws whose angles were not quite correct, and the judges bore strictly in mind the fact that screws are liable to a slight distortion after carving, due to the release of internal stresses in the timber, and also to the action of the polish. But even after making every possible consideration, the judges were constrained to reject screw No. 35 (C. J. Burchell), whose screw was one dram under weight, and whose pitch angles were incorrect with one another, neither of them conforming to the specified angle; No. 50 (A. E. Louch), which was under weight, but otherwise correct; No. 55 (V. Howes), under weight and incorrect pitch angles; and Nos. 61 and 53, incorrect angles. Competitors, as a general rule, had regarded the actual finishing of the screw as the end itself instead of the means to it, and only one screw strictly conformed to all the conditions. The limits allowed on weight were ample, but most of the competitors, it was noticed, worked to the low limit. Some confusion had occurred over the writer's statement that screws of a low weight would be under a disadvantage. That disadvantage was the possibility of disqualification. The rejected screws were carried right through the tests, however, so that the competitor should know exactly the performance made by his screw. In one instance, indeed, one of the rejected screws would undoubtedly have taken a prize had it conformed to the rules.

The fact that finish is of secondary importance is well brought to light by the excellent performance of screw No. 48 (L. Lansdowne), which was very badly finished, but of promising design for a beginner.

The judges were lenient regarding diameter, as this was against the competitor.

Method of Testing the Revolutions per Minute.—The revolutions per minute were first measured with the compressed-air container inflated to a pressure of 40 lb. to the square inch. The screw was timed for 15 secs. run at this pressure, and the revolutions taken by a special counter. The result was multiplied by four to give the revolutions per minute.

Experience with compressed air goes to show that the revolutions per minute obtained by this method are a fair index to the *average* revolutions per minute of the screw when the container is inflated to the pressure needed to obtain flight.

It is obvious that the higher the revolutions per minute the less would be the duration for a given pressure, and this fact had,

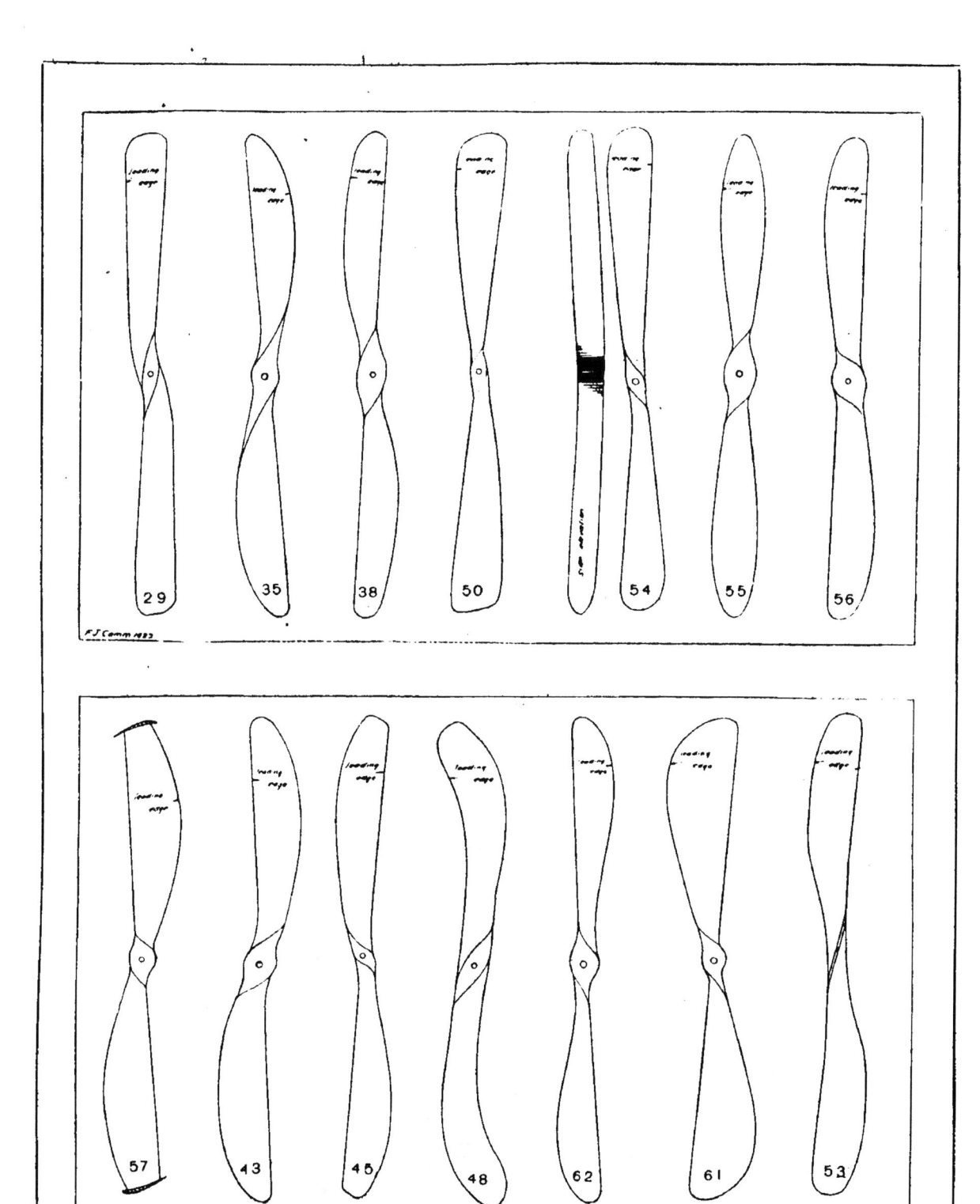

Outlines of the propellers entered for the competition; Nos. 62, 48, and 58 (not shown) were prize winners.

Table of Relative Air-Screw Efficiencies.

Name.	Screw No.	Weight.	Type.	Thrust.	Force Ft./lb.	Curved Edge.	R.P.M.	Pitch Angles.	Dia.	Blade Width.
G. A. Brown	29	9 drm.	Normale	6.73 oz.	630	---	996	O.K.	O.K.	1 1-16in
C. J. Burchell	35	7 drm.	Chauviere	6.72 oz.	629	Leading	961	Minus and blades not true with one another. (Rejected)	O.K.	1 3-16in
A. E. Whelpton	38	9 drm.	Chauviere	7.06 oz.	652	Leading	1032	Minus	O.K.	1 in.
J. E. Louch	50	7 drm.	Helical (rounded tips)	7.97 oz.	717	Trailing	861	O.K. (rejected)	O.K.	1¼ in.
G. Hayden	51	10 drm.	Helical (swept blades)	5.97 oz.	555	Trailing	940	O.K.	O.K.	1¼ in.
C. Howes	55	7 drm.	Elliptical	5.75 oz.	539	---	1012	O.K. (rejected)	O.K.	1¼ in.
S. H. Holton	56	14 drm.	Parallel blades	6.104 oz.	572	Trailing	904	O.K.	O.K.	1¼ in.
L. G. H. Hatful	57	15 drm.	Chauviere (rad. fins on tips)	4.71 oz.	441	Leading	860	O.K.	O.K.	1¼ in.
F. de P. Green	58	9 drm.	Chauviere (special fins)	7.06 oz.	662	Leading	900	Minus	¾ in. low	1 7-16 in.
C. A. Rippon	43	9 drm.	Chauviere	7.00 oz.	655	Trailing	868	O.K.	O.K.	1¼ in.
D. A. Pavely	45	9 drm.	Chauviere	5.64 oz.	529	Trailing	912	Minus	O.K.	1¼ in.
L. Lansdowne	48	9 drm.	S-type	7.28 oz.	681	---	920	O.K.	O.K.	1¼ in.
W. E. Evans	62	8 drm.	Chauviere	8.26 oz.	774	Leading	872	O.K.	O.K.	1¼ in.
R. E. Coleman	67	No. entry	---	---	---	---	---	---	---	---
H. A. B. Fryer	61	12 drm.	Helical	7.52 oz.	705	Leading	860	Minus (rejected)	O.K.	1¾ in.
S. C. Herson	53	9 drm.	Chauviere	8.27 oz.	775	Leading	956	Minus (rejected)	O.K.	1¼ in.

of course, to be taken into account, as the most efficient screw is that which, for a given torque, exerts the greatest thrust over the longest period. If time had not been taken into consideration it will readily be manifest that the screw with the highest revolutions per minute (tantamount to a high thrust spread over a very short period) would easily have been the winner.

Measuring the Thrust.—The container, inflated to a pressure of 60 lb. per square inch, with screw mounted, was suspended on a spring balance, the engine started, and the weight registered when the engine was running was deducted from the weight registered when it was stationary. This gave the maximum thrust. The judges were not satisfied, however, with the accuracy of this method, as the graduations on the balance were too small to accurately record half ounces, and postponed their final decision until fresh tests had been made. This was done at a later date on a thrust carriage of the form here shown, and devised by Mr. W. E. Evans. It will be seen that the container is freely suspended on a platform secured to long and fine wires from the ceiling. The container was inflated to the same pressure as before, and the horizontal distance moved by the platform measured by means of a rule placed on the bench top. This measurement was indicated by a tell-tale finger inserted in the platform, as shown. The total suspended weight was 5 lb., plus the weight of the screw, and it is obvious that the ratio between the horizontal distance moved due to thrust and the vertical height from the point of suspension to the point of measurement is the same as the ratio 'twixt the thrust and the weight. Expressed as a formula:

$$\text{Thrust} = \frac{\text{weight} \times \text{horizontal movement}}{\sqrt{\text{height}^2 - \text{horizontal movement}^2}}$$

Much finer results were made possible by this method, and thrust was calculated to two decimal places. Owing to the considerable length of the wires (90 in.) any inaccuracy of reading became correspondingly reduced in the calculation. Even an error in reading the horizontal movement of ⅛ in. (which, it need hardly be said, was in no instance made), would only make a difference of about 1/50 of an oz. It is, however, a tribute to the spring-balance method to note that the prizes would have been awarded to the same persons as by the thrust-carriage method. Where any doubt existed regarding a particular result, it was confirmed by a fresh test, and it may safely be concluded that the results of each screw presented in tabular manner herewith are extremely accurate.

Although the results given relate only to static thrust, it has been abundantly proved that with model screws this differs only to a very small degree with the dynamic thrust. As the power transmitted grows larger, of course, the discrepancy between static and dynamic thrust grows larger.

The Prize-winning Air-screws.—Mr. W. E. Evans' screw deservedly took first prize; it developed extremely high thrust at very low revolutions per minute, was very well finished, and was the only laminated screw entered. Great pains had undoubtedly been taken to adhere to the rules, for it agreed for diameter, weight, and angle.

With regard to Mr. Lansdowne's entry, the design undoubtedly has possibilities, and we should be glad to see a well-finished screw made. Mr. Lansdowne is only a tyro, so far as model aeronautics is concerned, but his screw (apart from finish) did conform to the rules.

The screw entered by Mr. Green, which is of a special nature (details of this cannot at present be divulged), although coming third, would undoubtedly have taken first or second prize had he not handicapped himself by making it of low diameter. The design has a future.

General Remarks.—A number of screws were entered with the curved edge *trailing* instead of leading, as is usual practice. Although the results obtained by them is by no means poor, they did not show up so well as the leading curved-edge ones, and we see no reason for the adoption of this practice.

Several screws would have undoubtedly put up a better performance had more attention been bestowed on the balance.

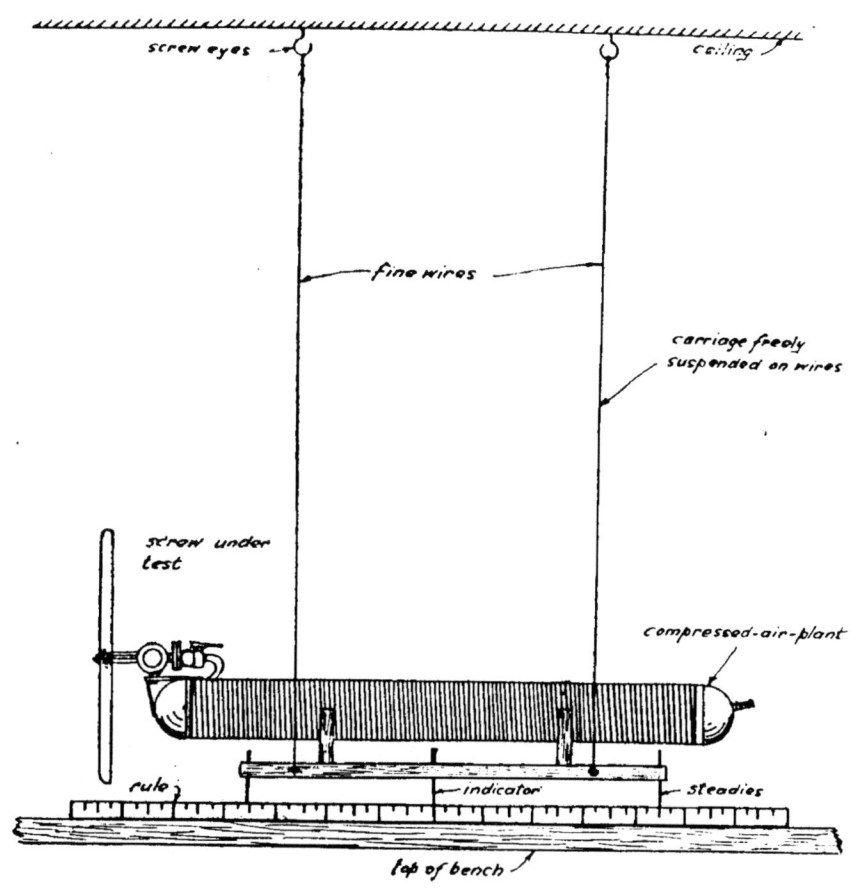

Apparatus for measuring static thrust of screws.

F.J. and Draughtsmanship and Handbooks

F.J.'s early successes stemmed from his aptitude for draughtsmanship and, no doubt, mathematics.

At school in Edwardian days he would be taught how to make working drawings for wood items – as Sydney had been at the Prince Albert Consort mechanics premises in Sheet Street, Windsor. The sections Sydney made are now in the R.A.F. Museum, Hendon. The conventions for architectural drawing differed from mechanical engineering drawing, especially when the latter became constricted by line work to be copied by the blue print process of 1900.

Timber tolerances were less precise than for mechanical engineering, and while work might be "offered up" until it fitted properly, dimensions measured by vernier gauge for example are necessary for manufacturing. Scaling off drawings would no longer be permissible for precision work. The rules and regulations were many and onerous, and F.J.'s *Drawing Office Practice* occupies 18 pages of the Engineer's Reference Book. Drawings for his wireless layouts could be pictorial representations.

F.J. anticipated the war time work of the Admiralty and Ministry of Production regarding draughtsmanship, and the latter became embodied in the British Standard 308 of 1953. His *Workshop Calculations Tables and Formulae* first published in 1938 contained much previously included in his *Workshop Arithmetic* of 1920 – one of the Cassell's *Work* handbooks. His 1938 handbook received a great demand for copies – especially from R.A.F. recruits who are reputed to have obtained Brownie points from its possession. It was reprinted annually for over ten editions. This handbook of about 150 pages deals with methods of calculation and the rules and formulae arising from workshop problems encountered by draughtsmen, engineering craftsmen, and of course, students.

The history of such matters stemmed from e.g. early motorcar manufacturing. His books on separate aspects such as *Screw Thread Tables, Screw Cutting, Dictionary of Metals and their Alloys, Gears and Gear Cutting*, also *Wire and Wire Gauges* were embodied in his mechanical engineering encyclopaedias and handbooks. Each was explained for the standard of a reader conversant with simple arithmetic in F.J.'s meticulous way of teaching.

Most of his illustrations are just that – illustrations, and not working drawings. His model aircraft designs were criticised (*C.S.R. Review* May 1949, Chapter 12) as representing the "state of the art" in the 1920s rather than later progress, and his preference for "spar" designs instead of the fuselage models as done in America did not suit all modellers. Some forcible letters are to be found in various publications as a result. On one occasion F.J. took umbrage and demanded – and received – a published letter of apology from the S.M.A.E. Editor, W.E. Evans. Thus: "With reference to the open letter which appeared in the May (1930) issue of this journal, I desire to withdraw any imputation which I may unwittingly have made against Mr F.J. Camm and I offer him my sincere apologies for the annoyance I have caused him. The letter was written on my own responsibility and in no way represented the views of the S.M.A.E. – W.E. Evans, Editor." (May 1930)

There were at least two other occasions (detailed later) when F.J. took action against his critics, and in each case he was successful (Greenly 1938/9) and Bernards Publishers Ltd (1944) both with costs and damages. F.J. could be abrasive.

F.J.'s Publishers

While George Newnes had published F.J.'s books and the journals he edited from about 1931 until his death in 1959, C. Arthur Pearson – who had published his *Flying Reference Book* in 1939/40 – had reappeared at Tower House, Southampton Street with F.J.'s *Home Electrician* in 1956, 1959 and 1962 and 1964 although the 1938 edition had been one of Newnes Home Mechanic books. The 1956 first edition has a note by F.J. "I am indebted to the publishers of *Practical Mechanics* for permission to use information and illustrations which appeared therein". What arrangement existed between George Newnes and C. Arthur Pearson – both of Tower House – is not known to me.

C. Arthur Pearson Ltd had their own "D.I.Y." series including *Do your own spray painting* by A. St. J. Masters, very much in the F.J. style.

F.J.'s earlier publishers had been Collins (1932, *The Book of Motors*), Sir I. Pitman's Motor-Cyclist Library in 1929 and 1930s.

Cassells Workshop Series published his *Mechanical Drawing* ("with others" in 1921, also *Model Aeroplanes* in the "Work" handbooks in 1920 and in the same year *Workshop Arithmetic.*

Hobbies (of Norfolk) New Annual had at least eight editions with F.J. as editor. F.J. became editor of *Hobbies* weekly, a "D.I.Y." publication in which he started out in 1929/30 a regular feature called "The practical wireless supplement". This quickly developed into George Newnes *Practical Wireless* in 1932. It was not the only "D.I.Y." wireless journal – there were at least eleven weeklies and eight monthly competitors which gradually fell by the wayside, as F.J.'s wireless articles – and free blue prints to build wireless sets – became increasingly popular and satisfactory. Some of these blue prints can be seen at the Amberley Chalk Pits Museum, Sussex, with the valves and parts that home constructors used.

Hobbies New Annuals are still treasured. The "Author's Foreword" for two editions are reproduced herewith, one is the Eighth, which can be dated 1933/4. His nephew is reputed to treasure all eight editions in Huddersfield ...

Author's Foreword

HOBBIES NEW ANNUAL makes its appearance for the eighth successive year, and in the present volume I have blended the contents according to the formula which has been found so successful in the seven previous issues—a success due chiefly to the fact that all the models, experiments, and apparatus described have actually been made before the text and illustrations were prepared. The generous use of illustrations is a much appreciated feature and so, too, is the fact that the construction work has been planned so that only a modest amount of skill and tool equipment are necessary.

The contents this year include a number of features not to be found in the previous issues; there are chapters on making a model dirigible; an automatic calendar; operating models from the mains (an important chapter, bearing in mind the growing interest in electrical mechanisms); staging a play at home; a ciné projector; a full-size sand yacht; chemical and electrical experiments; model aircraft; model railways; model boats; wireless; conjuring tricks; home-made telephone; a synchronous mains clock—these are but a few of the modern subjects herein treated. I would express my thanks to school teachers, headmasters, and other readers who have found my books of value to them in their work and hobbies and who have been kind enough to make suggestions for features for ensuing issues.

I should also like to set on record the fact that *Practical Mechanics*, the Sixpenny Monthly Journal of which I am the Editor, has, since the last issue of *Hobbies New Annual*, been placed on the approved list of recommended periodicals for use in Evening Classes and Schools by the London County Council.

F. J. CAMM.

Authors Foreword: Hobbies New Annual, 8th Year . (See Cover)

Author's Foreword

THE need for this comprehensive handbook is occasioned by the vast strides which have been made during the past five years in model aircraft. Formerly motive power was limited to elastic, although before the War one or two successful flights with petrol-driven models and also by those propelled by compressed air and steam had been achieved. Latterly, however, there has been an enormous revival in interest in large power-driven model aircraft, and this has been made possible by the production of several entirely reliable and trouble-free petrol engines of the two-stroke type, ranging in capacity from 2¼ c.c. to 15 c.c. These small engines weigh complete and in running order from 15 oz. to 20 oz., so that it is possible to build a model of from 4 ft. 6 in. to 8 ft. wing span and weighing from 3½ lb. to 8 lb. Flights of more than 50 miles have been attained by such petrol-driven models, and the record stands at 12 minutes 48 seconds (out of sight).

Elastic-driven models, too, have undergone a radical change, and the tendency nowadays is to build flying models which resemble full-size machines. Even these have been in the air for several minutes. It is impossible to state what the ultimate in duration will be, since under the present competition rules the model is timed from the moment of launching until it passes out of sight of the official timekeeper. Thus, a model which flies on a circular route within the vision of the timekeeper for, say, 3 minutes, can capture a record, whilst one which remains in sight for 2 mins. 59 secs., and then passes out of sight of the timekeeper, whilst still in the air, would not gain a record. I have no doubt that this rule will be changed perhaps by the time this book reaches the public.

I have endeavoured in this volume to deal with aspects of modern model aircraft, and it may therefore be considered as a supplementary volume to my companion works *Model Aeroplanes and Airships* and *Power-Driven Model Aircraft*, both of which are obtainable from the publishers of the present volume (address on page 4), for 1s. each, or by post for 1s. 2d. Those books have been very well received and many thousands of them have been sold. It is at the special request of readers of them that I have produced the present book, which may be regarded as a second course in advanced model aircraft construction. I have included in the last chapter constructional details of Mr. E. W. Twining's Primary Glider, since so many are graduating from petrol-driven aircraft to full-size work, and the glider forms a useful introduction to this. I wish to express my indebtedness to Mr. E. W. Twining. Might I draw readers' attention to the fact that *Practical Mechanics*, of which I am the Editor, and which is published monthly at 6d., contains a regular model aircraft feature and articles on full-size aircraft and gliding.

My thanks are also due to Capt. Bowden and others for letting me have photographs, details and descriptions of their models.

My advice is available to any reader who writes to me, c/o The Publishers, Messrs George Newnes, Ltd., Southampton Street, Strand, London, W.C.2, and encloses a stamped and addressed envelope.

F. J. CAMM

Authors Foreword: The Model Aircraft Book. (See Cover)

F.J. becomes an Editor

In 1918 he could claim to be "Model Editor of *Flight* and Technical Editor of *Everyday Science*".

Progressing from his competence as a draughtsman and because of his technical writing and painstaking research, he produced for Pitmans text books such as *The Book of the New Imperial Motor Cycle*, which at first he edited under the nom de plume of 'Waysider'. Next came the *Book of the BSA* motorcycle at first under his own name, but later under the name "Haycraft". These books ran into several editions.

F.J. appears to have been something of a freelance writer, as he also produced some "Work" handbooks for Cassell & Company, including *Model Aeroplanes, Mechanical Drawing* and their "Workshop" series, *Screw Cutting* 1920, and *Workshop Arithmetic* 1920. He was proud to find that *"Practical Mechanics, the Sixpenny monthly journal* of which I am the Editor, ... has been placed on the approved list of recommended periodicals for use in Evening Classes and Schools by the London County Council". (*Hobbies* New Annual 8).

His work was noted by Edward Malloy, the electrical expert at Pitmans, who when he left to become General Editor of the Technical Books Department at Newnes, invited F.J. to join him, producing Newnes Home Mechanic books. The first of these was *The Home Woodworker* followed by *Model Aeroplanes and Airships* (the work of F.J. being apparent). Then came *25 Simple Working Models* – "with other volumes in preparation." These successes arose from F.J. becoming Editor of *New Hobbies* which seems to have dealt with every hobby and handcraft. A blurb refers to "*Model Aeroplanes and Gliders, Electric Motors, Model Trains, Furniture, Musical Instruments, Stamp Collecting, Amateur Photography* and general work in wood and metal." There was a section dealing with wireless, and this was to expand tremendously and take up much of F.J.'s time. With a "Free Advice" offer – a bureau that F.J. incorporated in all his journals in later days – *New Hobbies* – at 2d per week – less than one penny – sold briskly, and Camm fans grew in number. The designs were such as "could be made with a minimum of expense, and without an elaborate tool kit" – and even a suitable kit was obtainable for free by regular buyers of the journal. Not all his designs were appreciated – one correspondent informed me that he tried to build an electric motor from a cocoa tin, as described by F.J. – which refused to work ...

Articles were reused – after revision – for books, and might be collected into encyclopaedias and Annuals, as with *Hobbies New Annual*. These show his interests on the fly leaf. Thus, a *Hobbies New Annual* (undated) state that he was "F.R.S.A., Editor of *Practical Mathematics, The Cyclist, Bicycling News, Practical and Amateur Wireless* (Newnes amalgamated with Cassells *Amateur Wireless* in 1934), and *Practical Motorist. Amateur Wireless* had grown out of *Everyday Science*. This was also edited by F.J. Camm, whose *Marvels of Modern Science* appeared in 1935, and a revised edition in 1938. His principal groups of writing concerned wireless, mathematics, mechanics, cycling, motoring, workshop processes – and household matters, including electricity, also workshop arithmetic, workshop calculations, and formulae.

Wireless Telegraphy

Patrick Y. Alexander had brought some knowledge about "wireless" to Windsor – he had once worked with Sir Oliver Lodge, who had demonstrated wireless telegraphy at the Royal Institution, but saw his work only as an extension of the laws of electro-magnetic radiation.

There had been some journals with articles on transmission, and morse signals, but in September 1914 the government banned the use of wireless apparatus by amateurs. This ban was not lifted until December 1918. Previously Henry Greenly had been interested in the subject – and young F.J. Camm, who had become Technical Writer for Henry Greenly's *Models, Railways and Locomotives* in June 1918, and then Editor, Model Flying Machines in *Everyday Science* which had merged with M.R. & L. It seems possible that F.J.'s interest in wireless and telegraphy would benefit from working with Henry Greenly.

The subject had attracted amateurs who could obtain apparatus from such stores as A.W. Gamages of Holborn, as listed in their catalogue *The Home Scientist* in 1914.

Previously interest had been drawn to wireless communication by the arrest of the murderer Dr Crippen in 1911, when messages to and from the liner Montrose sailing to Quebec resulted in Crippen and his paramour Ethel Le Neve – dressed as a boy – being arrested on arrival by Inspector Dew who had crossed in the faster Laurentic. Detective stories were as popular then as now!

The possibilities of wireless were emphasised in 1912 when the great liner TITANIC broadcast urgent signals as it sank on its maiden voyage.

All Windsor knew of the tragedy because a Windsor telegraph boy, Owen Allum, was on board en route to his father in New York. He was drowned, and his body was taken to New York and then returned to Windsor for burial at Clewer Church. This was unusual – very few of those drowned were brought back to this country. Clewer Churchyard was packed for the funeral, and F.J. would have been impressed – by the importance of the morse code. He emphasised this later when pointing out the need to know morse when seeking a transmission licence.

The 1914-18 war produced great progress regarding wireless and small transmitting stations were established including in 1922 the British Broadcasting Company with 2LO. D.I.Y. sets – mostly crystal sets – became common. School boys wound coils and swapped "variometers" and aerials appeared everywhere. By 1925 there were two million licences – at ten shillings (50p) per annum. Factory built sets were expensive and could be unreliable. F.J. said "Anyone who builds a crystal set became an acknowledged expert". The day of the Do It Yourself wireless set had arrived.

Wireless Telegraphy Tuition

The great Marconi had founded the Wireless Telegraphy and Signals Company in New Street, Chelmsford in 1899 – the first purpose-built wireless station in the world. Even the Chancellor of the Exchequer Lloyd George speculated in Marconi shares – but only in American companies – so he was forgiven.

Practical Wireless reported the work of many local radio clubs including one at Windsor, F.J.'s home town. F.J. was interested in the EAST BERKSHIRE COLLEGE RADIO SOCIETY, which met at the Royal Albert Institute, Sheet Street, Windsor, Honorary Secretary F.H. Rickard, A.M.J.P.R.E. This was formed at the end of September 1954. The club transmitter call sign was G3/KAL. The facilities included a club room, extensive equipment and technical film shows, also lectures – such as F.J. gave in those days. (Reported by *Practical Wireless* in March 1955). Courses at Windsor included a three year course for the intermediate and final certificates of the City & Guilds of London Institute in Radio Service Work. There was also a Radio Amateur's Licence course of the R.A.I. for those who intended to obtain from the Post Master General an amateur's transmitting licence. This required Morse training as well as practical work.

There was growing interest in short wave wireless, with its world wide scope and amateur transmitting was encouraged by F.J.

The Morse Code was essential knowledge for obtaining a wireless transmission licence so F.J. included the code in his *Wireless Constructor's Encyclopaedias*. Whenever a wireless receiver aerial was erected – even if not connected to a receiver – a Post Office Licence costing ten shillings (50p) was required. In addition, if the receiver used any of Marconi's Wireless Telegraph patents, a licence from Marconi was required, and a plate had to be exhibited on the set stating that royalties had been paid. Marconi charged 12 shillings and six pence per valve used, (62^1/$_2$ pence.) These constrictions soon passed.

His *Short-Wave Manual*, published in 1942, reached the U.S. Army Library indexed as "A treatise on the design, construction, operation and adjustment of short and ultra-short-wave receivers, aerials and equipment". It contains designs for building eight different short wave receivers and information for "constructing your own coils in detail". (213 pages, 118 illustrations).

F.J.'s book *Wireless Transmission*, reported as "An ideal book for the Amateur" cost six shillings (30p) and by 1955 was in its eighth edition. This was the year that F.J. was photographed at the blackboard, apparently surrounded by a class of students, and giving a lecture on radio. He was posing for his latest reprint, *A Beginner's Guide to Radio*, where the picture appears on the dust jacket. The reprint was based upon his very popular series of articles in *Practical Wireless* over two years. F.J.'s lecture at the National Book Week, Felixstowe in 1955, attracted considerable attention in the press.

F.J. noted in 1955 the first portable radio frames that gave acoustic information about, e.g. water mains under the pavement – and that "strong radio waves are being received from an unknown spot on Jupiter, 500 million miles away. A radio telescope was being constructed to find out more about these mysterious signals".

In 1938 F.J.'s *Wireless Transmission for Amateurs* sold well, and he included a simple one valve transmitter in his *Wireless Constructors Encyclopaedia*. Amateur short wave transmissions resulted in wireless "pen" pals across the world and amateur call sign cards were exchanged. King Hussein of Jordan being a keen short wave transmitter, his card holds pride of place in many collections.

Anecdotes of urgent messages lose nothing in the telling. One refers to the 1947 Thames flood, when an accident at Welley Corner near Windsor occurred – a lorry carrying evacuees ran off the road. No telephones were working, but an amateur radio fan of F.J.'s who lived nearby sent out a call for help. This was picked up in Italy, where another amateur telephoned the police in London – who passed the message on to Slough. (But by then help had already reached the stranded party).

F.J. introduced new circuits and terms to amateurs. Their abbreviations Super heterodyne, class "B" and other forms of Push Pull amplification came into common used, with complex valves including "single Diode Tetrode, Double Diode Tetrodes (and pentodes) until commercial receivers took over from the D.I.Y. amateur, who however continued to experiment, and read F.J.'s guiding notes on progress.

The Home Electrician

F.J. had realised that the increasing use of electrical labour saving devices in the home had brought a need for "advice to the handy man repairer". The Home Office regulation that no one, save an authorised person over the age of 21 be allowed to interfere with an electrical installation, may not be generally known nor that an Electrical Inspector must be allowed to inspect an installation before being connected to the mains. These safety rules were emphasised in his book *The Home Electrician* in 1956. Apart from this, he included advice on home made burglar alarms, water heating, electric models run from the mains, and repairs to common household appliances.

The 1955 Silver Jubilee Radio Show at Earls Court was opened by F.J.'s friend Lord Brabazon. The review published in *Practical Wireless* was prepared by his old friend Lord Donegal, the Marquis of Donegal.

George Newnes popular magazine *Practical Wireless* originally edited by F.J., celebrated its 60 years of publication in 1992, with a special edition researched by Mrs Joan Ham of Storrington, entitled *The Man behind it all – F.J. Camm*. This related the saga of the journal, and of F.J. who wrote handbooks for every section of wireless-circuits, short wave sets, superhets, coils, chokes, valves, and various types of transmitter and receiver. These he collected into *The Wireless Constructors Encyclopaedia* which was purchased by 60,000 readers, and such was the success that it was reprinted again after several editions as *The News Chronicle Wireless Constructors Encyclopaedia*. This had to be reprinted in several more

Practical Wireless

Published Weekly

Volume I.

September 24th, 1932, to March 18th, 1933

(Nos. 1 — 26)

Editor:

F. J. CAMM

London:
George Newnes, Ltd., 8-11, Southampton Street,
Strand, W.C.2

editions. These books are still avidly collected. About this time the term 'Camm's Comics' became a term of tribute and not derogatory, and related to his visually appealing layouts.

Free blue-prints were offered from time to time, examples being the "Long Range Three" and "The Superhet Three" – to be built for less than £5. The Royal Silver Jubilee was marked by "The All Wave Silver Souvenir" covering long, medium and short wave bands. One of the last of the pre-war designs was the "Push-Button Four" with F.J. pictured on the cover of the journal.

Every project was tested – they also tested commercial kits – and every effort was made to improve standards of components and layouts. The F.J. free advice bureau was behind these offers, so that satisfaction was assured.

The team of experts behind F.J. was his strength, and in addition he could call upon other experts for articles, one being the Marquis of Donegal – whose Best Man and friend he was – although on one occasion the Marquis's *Practical Mechanics* article on the "Factories of South Wales", and later "Long Distance Telephones" generated some critical letters as he seems to have overlooked the British Post

Office Telephones use of "two voiced-frequency" trunk signalling and dialling system (known as 2V-F) from 1940.

It is a long story from early crystal sets with earphones followed by sets with glowing valves and accumulators – charged at the local garage and liable to leak acid, also the heavy dry batteries with cells soldered together to give the voltage required by horn loud speakers, and the early mains sets that hummed and crackled. Improvements were steadily made, power increased and size and weight of sets reduced until reliability could be taken for granted.

Some vintage "F.J." blue-prints and wireless sets and components are displayed at the Amberley Museum, West Sussex, which is well worth a visit.

On Your Wavelength — By Thermion

Thirty-one Years of Service!

THIS issue celebrates 21 years of continuous publication under one editor, Mr. F. J. Camm. I cannot claim to have served PRACTICAL WIRELESS for that period. I have sailed under two flags—*Amateur Wireless* from November 18th, 1922, until it succumbed to the fierce opposition of P.W., which absorbed it with its issue, dated January 26th, 1935. Mine was one of the few features which was carried on in the combined journal which, for a time, appeared under the title of *Practical and Amateur Wireless*. I well remember the sadness of the parting with my old love and the regret with which I received the news that a new journal, after a short space of three years, had knocked out the older of the two first radio journals. I remember, too, the smirks which took place in the editorial office of *Amateur Wireless* when it was first announced in *World's Press News* and other trade journals that George Newnes, Ltd., had decided to enter the highly competitive field of radio; we all gave it about three months, in view of the fact that in 1932, when "P.W." was launched, a large number of weekly and monthly competitors had had a ten-year start. I do not think that the editors of contemporaries enjoyed the same nonchalance and also *sang-froid*, because they planned boom issues to coincide with the first issue of P.W. The daily newspapers carried announcements singing not only the virtues of the new, but the praises of the old.

To have been first in many cases proves nothing but antiquity. To have become first and to have slain in honest combat most of the old established rivals is an achievement as far as I know without parallel in the history of periodical journalism.

The first issue of *Amateur Wireless* was dated June 10th, 1922, but I was not invited to contribute my weekly critique until the issue dated November 18th, 1922. Under the rules which then applied, a restraining hand was placed upon my comments and quite often my remarks were considered hyper-critical and watered down by the time they appeared in print. The merging of the two journals did not occasion any hiatus. *Amateur Wireless* was suitably interred on January 19th, 1935, and combined with P.W. the following week, which carried the first of my contributions under the new editorship.

When I was called to the editorial sanctum sanctorum of PRACTICAL WIRELESS, I was pleasantly surprised to find that only the mildest of editorial restraint would be placed upon my writings, no doubt with a lively eye to the law of libel. I must say I found it refreshing to meet an editor whose only interest was his readers and who believed not in the write-up and trade puff adopted by so many journals, and in which things which quite rightly ought to be severely criticised are praised, but in honest criticism without punches being pulled.

In carrying out this policy, I must say that brickbats and bouquets quite often have been deposited on my desk. Some readers have not seen eye to eye with me, whilst others have enjoined me to be even more critical. No critic worthy of his salt can expect to write that with which every one of his readers will agree. If he does he is only expressing the obvious and his writings are merely space-filling froth. How often does it occur that contributors have to serve under nervous editors who will hint at a fault and hesitate dislike—being willing to wound and yet afraid to strike! Such journals can never be taken seriously and, in the long run, their opinions will be accepted *cum grano salis*.

It was in such an atmosphere of keen competitive journalism that I witnessed one by one the old established journals fall by the wayside, until to-day only one esteemed competitor of long standing remains. It is not given to many contributors to write one feature continuously for 31 years and by this time, I think, I can fairly claim to be the doyen of radio journalists, for I was writing about radio long before the foundation of any of the popular radio journals. This issue, therefore, provides me with the occasion for a double celebration, and over my glass of sarsaparilla I shall toast not only my editor and colleagues, but my fellow contributors and the thousands of friends and friendly enemies who continue to write to me—yes even those whom, from time to time, ask the editor to sack me.

I am touched by the esteem, almost amounting to reverence, in which I am held by some readers; and by the belief in the omniscience with which some think I can solve their troubles. It is true that, in the course of years I have acted as intermediary for readers who have felt, perhaps, that some advertiser has not dealt fairly with them. Those have been rare occasions, but in every case I have found the advertiser has an adequate answer and satisfaction has always been obtained. All technical journals to-day run a light feature as a sort of comic relief to the technicalities of other pages. My feature is intended to provide a source of gentle bandinage and persiflage on this, that and the other and to criticise, choosing fair words. If I have not succeeded in the passage of 31 years in pleasing all of my readers all of the time I can at least claim to have pleased most of them most of the time.

I must say that I have loved writing this feature above all of my other journalistic work and I hope I shall be allowed to continue to do so.

My gratitude to all those readers who have written congratulatory messages.

Also to the many hundreds of beginners who have written to me on the subject of pictorial v. theoretical circuits; the general concensus of opinion is that we should give both, and steps are being taken in that direction. A selection of readers' opinions is to be published.

"On Your Wavelength" by Thermion

F.J. used the pseudonym "Thermion" for 31 years, and "claimed to be the doyen of radio journalists".

The first issue of *Amateur Wireless* was dated 10th June 1922. In November 1922 F.J. was invited to contribute – but this proved to be under considerable editorial restraint.

When *Practical Wireless* was started by George Newnes on 24th September 1932, F.J. appears to have been among the pessimists to expected Newnes to fail.

Before 1929, both F.J. and Edward Molloy worked for Pitmans, then Molloy went to George Newnes as General Editor, Technical Books Department. He persuaded F.J. to join him in George Newnes, and F.J. became editor of *Hobbies*, a weekly D.I.Y. journal. F.J. soon started a *Practical Wireless Supplement* which became the forerunner of *Practical Wireless* on 24th September 1932. When *Amateur Wireless* merged with *Practical Wireless* in 1935 and forthwith F.J. was invited to become Editor of the combined journal – a position he held for the rest of his life.

Thus, F.J. had 37 years of service concerning wireless, including 27 years as Editor of *Practical Wireless*, with his name on the cover of the magazine.

F.J. started a page headed "Thoughts of Thermion" which appeared in every *Practical Wireless* journal until his death. These tended to reveal his character and characteristics – he was a No Nonsense man, anti Hot Gospellers and a purist for pronunciation, critical sometimes about the regional accents of BBC regional broadcasting stations. Americanisms displeased him and the affectations whereby "O" was pronounced "U" (as in Compton the cricketer and Montgomery, Field Marshall).

His popular *Beginner's Guide to Radio* was published in Braille by the Royal National Institute.

H.J. Barton Chapple was F.J.'s assistant from the first issue and one of the technical staff of *Practical Wireless* in 1932. He was highly qualified, and designed a great many sets for *Practical Wireless*, the "Argus Three" being very popular. It could be purchased as a kit from Direct Radio for £8.13.0d complete with three valves and a cabinet, or for £5.2.6d without valves, £8.65 and £5.12$^{1}/_{2}$ respectively.

Practical Wireless

F.J. published several pages of *Practical Wireless* history in the October 1953 edition commencing with "A Brief History of its Inception and Development" by the Editor. It would be presumptuous for me to try to summarise F.J.'s own words, which are included verbatim. This is followed by his "Milestones 1932-1953" and the Editorial he wrote to celebrate "our 21st Birthday".

Practical Television and F.J. Camm

There had been test transmissions by John Logie Baird (the inventor) in 1925 with his mechanically scanned T.V. and in 1929 from the Baird company's studios in Long Acre, London. Broadcasts continued with the BBC 2L0 station – then on the roof of Selfridges' store. The BBC charged £5 per half hour for the use of the transmitters.

The BBC started their own transmissions on 22nd August 1932. In August 1936 there were transmissions from Alexander Palace, the Baird and the better Marconi-E.M.I. systems being used on alternate days. By November 1936 regular transmissions were being made. These were by 30 line mechanical scanning disc televisors, which were reputed to be capable of being built from vacuum sweeper motors and neon tubes "for a few shillings". The *Daily Express* promoted a receiver costing £5 approximately for BBC medium wave transmissions. F.J. included nearly 24 pages of illustrated details on the theory of building and testing a receiver in his *Wireless Constructor's Encyclopaedia* sponsored by the *News Chronicle*. This went into several editions.

The 1939-45 war closed down television.

Practical Wireless, November 7th, 1932 – The "Argus 3"

Twenty-one Years of "P.W." Progress

A BRIEF HISTORY OF ITS INCEPTION AND
DEVELOPMENT   By The Editor

THE first issue of PRACTICAL WIRELESS appeared on September 24th, 1932. The first public broadcasting service took place in 1922 under the auspices of the British Broadcasting Company (call sign 2LO), which later became the British Broadcasting Corporation. Thus, when this journal was launched, radio had been in existence for 10 years, and the industry was only just getting into its stride. Long before 1922, however, the amateur movement in this country had developed and gained a strong footing. The experimental station at Writtle (call sign 2MT) had been broadcasting a half an hour's programme once a week for some time previously. It was a programme keenly looked forward to by amateur set builders who only had this brief period once a week to test new receivers or check alterations to old ones.

Captain P. P. Eckersley was the chief engineer of Writtle and he later, of course, became chief engineer of the British Broadcasting Company. In those days he was very much a general factotum, for apart from the problems associated with that early transmitter, he had to arrange programmes and often act as announcer.

Prior to the installation of Writtle the amateur movement in this country, carefully fostered by the Radio Society of Great Britain, was entirely confined to amateur transmitters, and a tribute must be paid to this society for the pioneer work it did and still continues to do. For it was from the pool of amateurs that the industry drew its personnel. Many of these pioneer amateurs founded businesses of their own.

The first "Practical Wireless," dated September 24th, 1932.

It will be seen that amateur set constructors have been the basis upon which the radio industry was founded. In 1922 when the first daily service was introduced a wave of enthusiasm for the new hobby spread over the country. In the remotest village lone experimenters built crystal sets and, if they were a little more ambitious, one- and two-valve sets, and made a profitable hobby out of building for their friends.

In those days literature which could be read and understood by amateurs was scant. There was only one regular periodical whilst a few of the journals dealing with technical subjects for amateurs devoted a page or so a week to the new national hobby. Firms in their hundreds started up to supply components for this new market, and it was not long before publishers saw that radio, quite apart from being the flash in the pan which hitherto they thought it would be, was here to stay and develop, and that it would become eventually an inseparable part of our national life, like boots, bedsteads and bicycles.

It was not many months after 2LO started that two popular journals appeared, and within the short space of two years there was a large number of weekly and monthly radio journals. Each had large circulations and performed a good service in fostering interest in the new hobby and in reporting on the latest technical developments.

It was not long before complete sets appeared on the market and it was thought at that time that this would spell the doom of home construction. Instead of that it acted as a fillip; for the complete receivers were sold only to those who were unable to build receivers through lack of elementary technical skill. The ranks of constructors continued to grow during the 10 years which

---

GREETINGS FROM LORD BURGHLEY

(*President, Radio Industry Council.*)

Congratulations to PRACTICAL WIRELESS *on attaining its 21st birthday and good wishes for continued success in stimulating and maintaining wide interest among its readers. In 21 years there has grown up a vital radio industry.*

Although technical progress has been almost overwhelming to the layman, the subject of wireless somehow retains its early romantic interest and it is easy to see why it remains a fascinating and satisfying hobby for so many.

Practical Wireless — The Editor's Brief History

preceded the publication of this journal. They thrived and each produced during each year number of " boom " sets supported by a fr blueprint.

In those days any man who built a crystal set beca an acknowledged expert. Books poured from presses and the periodicals issue by issue describe some new receiver or improvements to old ones.

" Practical Wireless " is Born

It was in such an atmosphere that PRACTICAL WIRELESS was born, but it is necessary to go bac before the date of its first issue to trace the seed fro which it germinated.

I was the founder Editor of PRACTICAL WIRELESS but prior to that I was also the Editor of *Hobbie* a weekly journal appealing to handymen. Th readers of that journal made it quite clear to me th whilst they were interested in woodwork, mod boats, model aeroplanes and locomotives, and t other practical hobbies, they would welcome a weekl feature devoted to radio. Accordingly, in the issu of that journal dated February 13th, 1932, I com menced a weekly radio feature under the title o " The Practical Wireless Supplement." In it wa described a number of simple circuits mostly of th detector and 2 L.F. type, which were built in larg numbers. From the volume of correspondence which accrued it soon became evident that the part coul not contain the whole, and that it would be necessary to start a separate weekly publication. This was a bold venture when it is remembered that there were 11 weeklies and eight monthly competitors with a 10 years' start. It had become apparent, however, that the trade would support a new weekly running on different lines, and it was as a result of discussions with members of the trade after a very careful survey of the publishing possibilities that the decision was taken in July, 1932, to produce PRACTICAL WIRELESS.

PRACTICAL WIRELESS was the last journal in the field, but it is an obvious tribute to the soundness of its policy, which does not need stressing, that most of its competitors fell by the wayside within a few years, until to-day only one remains and that the first and oldest.

Our Policy

The policy of the paper is well known to all older readers and to the trade. We decided to produce designs for receivers which readers could build with absolute confidence that they would perform in accord with the stated claims. We would specify only the actual parts to be used in our receivers without any eye to advertising revenue, and irrespective of whether the manufacturers of the components advertised or not.

The solus specification has remained part of our editorial policy ever since and we do not propose to depart from it. We introduced, to back up that policy, our Free Advice Bureau, in the belief that every reader who built a set from our pages was entitled to the same free advisory service that he would obtain had he bought a commercial receiver.

Naturally there was fluttering in the dovecotes of our contemporaries when the news was announced in the trade press that yet another constructor's journal was to appear. Members of the trade were informed that it could not last, and we met with the fiercest opposition when the first issue in a red and blue cover appeared on that day 21 years ago when the first issue of this journal was launched, with a free gift blueprint of our very first receiver—The Long Range Express Three. Up to that time most amateur sets were designed for baseboard construction. Such sets looked amateurish, and because all of the components were located on one plane they were large in size. The Long Range Express was one of the first, if not the first, of the amateur sets to make use of a metal chassis, thus reducing its bulk and enabling unsightly components to be tucked away out of sight in the sub-chassis.

Each of our designs was well tried and tested before it saw the light of print. In many cases we led design and encouraged manufacturers to produce components of newer types and improved performance.

Thus, on September 24th, 1932, every radio-minded enthusiast in this country was appraised, by means of large advertisements in most of the national and provincial newspapers and by means of posters in the newsagents' shops, that the first issue of a new and improved constructor's journal had been launched.

Gift Offers

The first issue of PRACTICAL WIRELESS also contained a remarkable book offer. Every reader who took the paper regularly could obtain a copy, upon payment of a very small sum, of the *Wireless Constructor's Encyclopædia* (now the *Practical Wireless Encyclopædia*). Over 60,000 readers availed themselves of that offer, which was later repeated by the *News Chronicle*, whose readers absorbed a further 50,000 copies. To-day that book is in its 12th edition and over 300,000 copies have been sold throughout the world. This does not take into account editions printed in other languages such as Spanish.

To make good an obvious omission in the technical literature of radio we also undertook the preparation of a whole series of handbooks which would appeal to the amateur, and to date over 40 of them have appeared—each having run through many editions.

The pages of PRACTICAL WIRELESS have promptly recorded each new development in radio, often long ahead of its competitors. It went from strength to strength, its circulation steadily increasing and gaining prestige issue by issue. Within three years it was firmly established and the first sign of a crack in the front of its competitors appeared in the announcement in the daily press which was headed " Two Famous Journals Combine." This preceded the statement that as from issue dated January 26th, 1935, *Amateur Wireless* would be merged with PRACTICAL WIRELESS. The second oldest of the popular weeklies had collapsed, and for a time this journal appeared as *Practical and Amateur Wireless*. That journal had grown, like PRACTICAL WIRELESS, out of a supplement to another journal—*Everyday Science*, of which I was also the Editor. *Amateur Wireless* was published by Cassell & Company. The departure of our competitors, however, was not the signal for us to relax our efforts, indeed, we increased them, and for the next six years we continued to appear weekly and in the larger size of pre-war years.

Size Reduction

The declaration of war in 1939 and the restriction on paper supplies naturally caused us in common with all other journals to reduce the number of pages in each issue, but we continued to appear weekly in our pre-war size until July 27th, 1940, and as a monthly in that same size until November, 1941. The first issue of PRACTICAL WIRELESS in the present size was dated December, 1941. Naturally, the editorial policy of the war years was veered to suit the changed conditions. The Services required thousands of technical personnel as radio telegraphists and radio and radar operators, and we therefore commenced publication of articles of an educational nature.

Adequate tribute has been paid to the services we rendered to the State in this connection, and we continue to receive letters of gratitude from those now holding prominent positions in the Services and in the radio industry, for the instruction they received at our hands and which was responsible for their progress.

Except for the printers' strike in 1950 which compelled us to produce two issues in one (dated September-October, 1950), we have appeared continuously, and to date 564 issues have been despatched all over the world from this office. For PRACTICAL WIRELESS has a world-wide circulation, and we daily receive letters from almost every part of the globe. Messages of congratulation have poured in since the announcement some months ago of this Special Birthday Number from thousands of readers who have taken the paper from its first issue.

Other pages in this issue date-line the milestones in our history and list some of our most famous receivers. Earlier readers, however, will remember our introduction of Transfer prints by means of which, like a ladies' embroidery pattern, the wiring diagram could be imprinted on the chassis; our free gift Wire Gauge and set of B.A. Spanners; our free gift Data Sheets and Booklets; our Pocket Tool Kits, to mention but a few of our efforts to assist constructors.

"Practical Television"

As we pass the twenty-first milestone we observe the same enthusiasm for television as permeated radio in its early years. Instead of having to cramp this new branch of electronics into a small section of this journal it now has our sister journal "Practical Television" to cater for the needs of the amateur. The next twenty-one years will see marked changes in both of these allied sciences, and readers may rely on this journal promptly and accurately to record those developments and to bring to them, as hitherto, news from the four quarters of the earth. We express our sincere thanks to them, and to our advertisers for their loyalty and their continued support.

The great fire of 30th November 1936 which destroyed the Crystal Palace also speeded the collapse of the original Baird T.V. manufactory. John Logie Baird occupied part of the south tower, also adjoining buildings where he invented, and had a cathode ray tube manufactory, also laboratories. Only the cathode ray stock pile was saved, noted F.J.

Practical Mechanics own electrical expert in the F.J. coterie, H.J. Barton Chapple, detailed in February 1934 the Baird and the BBC system mechanical scanning device of those days for experimental television, when the cathode ray tube was becoming available.

It was not long before F.J. published his D.I.Y. book.

1936 was the year that F.J. included *Practical Television* in the title of *Practical Wireless*. His first television and short wave manual had been offered to readers in 1934, when *Practical Television* was launched. He reviewed the first commercial television receivers in 1936, when the BBC television service was introduced. Those who subscribed to Baird's £100,000 T.V. flotation probably lost their money. The BBC changed over to the E.M.I. system. In 1943 F.J. reported that Baird was able to introduce colour television. Baird was to die in 1946, the year that the BBC T.V. Service recommenced after the war. F.J. was impressed deeply by John Logie Baird's early T.V. achievements – the scanning disc machine was a scientific toy. The opening of the first of a chain of T.V. stations resulted in the T.V. section of *Practical Wireless* having to expand into the *Practical Television* companion journal first published on 24th March 1950.

One of F.J.'s articles in 1935 included "Directions for Television Made Easy" – typical of his enthusiasm for his subject.

His *Beginner's Guide to Television* cost seven shillings and 6d (37^1/$_2$p) and was a companion volume to his *Beginner's Guide to Radio*. This was an elementary course in 27 lessons. Published annually for three or four years, the fourth edition was published after his death in 1959.

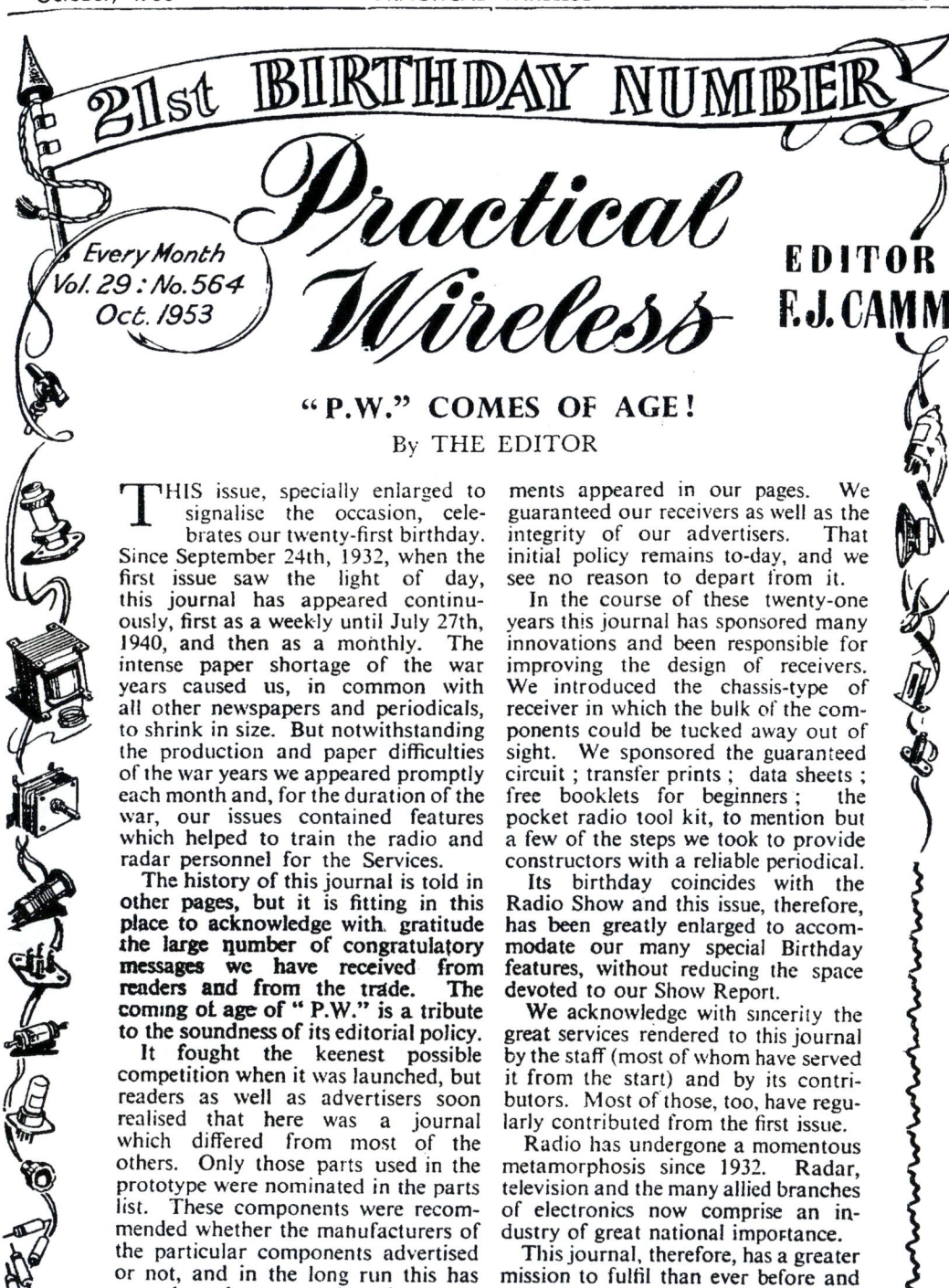

21st BIRTHDAY NUMBER
Practical Wireless

Every Month
Vol. 29 : No. 564
Oct. 1953

EDITOR
F. J. CAMM

"P.W." COMES OF AGE!
By THE EDITOR

THIS issue, specially enlarged to signalise the occasion, celebrates our twenty-first birthday. Since September 24th, 1932, when the first issue saw the light of day, this journal has appeared continuously, first as a weekly until July 27th, 1940, and then as a monthly. The intense paper shortage of the war years caused us, in common with all other newspapers and periodicals, to shrink in size. But notwithstanding the production and paper difficulties of the war years we appeared promptly each month and, for the duration of the war, our issues contained features which helped to train the radio and radar personnel for the Services.

The history of this journal is told in other pages, but it is fitting in this place to acknowledge with gratitude the large number of congratulatory messages we have received from readers and from the trade. The coming of age of " P.W." is a tribute to the soundness of its editorial policy.

It fought the keenest possible competition when it was launched, but readers as well as advertisers soon realised that here was a journal which differed from most of the others. Only those parts used in the prototype were nominated in the parts list. These components were recommended whether the manufacturers of the particular components advertised or not, and in the long run this has proved to be a sound policy. We took particular care to see that only straightforward advertisers announcements appeared in our pages. We guaranteed our receivers as well as the integrity of our advertisers. That initial policy remains to-day, and we see no reason to depart from it.

In the course of these twenty-one years this journal has sponsored many innovations and been responsible for improving the design of receivers. We introduced the chassis-type of receiver in which the bulk of the components could be tucked away out of sight. We sponsored the guaranteed circuit ; transfer prints ; data sheets ; free booklets for beginners ; the pocket radio tool kit, to mention but a few of the steps we took to provide constructors with a reliable periodical.

Its birthday coincides with the Radio Show and this issue, therefore, has been greatly enlarged to accommodate our many special Birthday features, without reducing the space devoted to our Show Report.

We acknowledge with sincerity the great services rendered to this journal by the staff (most of whom have served it from the start) and by its contributors. Most of those, too, have regularly contributed from the first issue.

Radio has undergone a momentous metamorphosis since 1932. Radar, television and the many allied branches of electronics now comprise an industry of great national importance.

This journal, therefore, has a greater mission to fulfil than ever before and with this twenty-first Birthday number it dedicates itself anew to its readers and the trade:—F. J. C.

Practical Wireless 21st Birthday Number Editorial

My 21 Years as Editor
1932 — By F. J. Camm — 1953

AS in the case of human beings, so with a periodical, the completion of 21 years of existence is considered an occasion for celebration. It "comes of age." It provides me with an opportunity of dispensing with the editorial "we" and adopting the style of personal narrative—also with an opportunity for retrospection.

The years slip past unnoticed, and it scarcely seems possible that 21 years have elapsed since I passed the proofs of the first issue, which was published on September 24th, 1932. During those 21 years I have had little time for reflection or retrospection, but now that I can relax for a moment I can look back with justifiable pride on 21 years of successful achievement.

A glance at the bookshelves in my office provides reminders of my output during that time. I recall a comment made by the editor of a well-known encyclopaedia when the first bound copies of his work were placed on his desk: "Did I *really* produce all that?" For in those 21 years I have written over 21,000,000 words, and probably far more, in the form of articles and books. This represents an output of over 20,000 words a week, apart from the work of make-up, proof-reading, arranging exhibitions, lectures, and the other general work associated with the work of an editor.

It is evident, therefore, that I have "shunned delight and lived laborious days," but they have been pleasant days. I have made a hobby of work. I believe in it, and I do not like holidays. I believe that "the best of all ways to lengthen your days is to steal a few hours from the night." I have devoted all of those 21 years with energy and enthusiasm to this and our associated journals, and I have not spared myself. The task has been enjoyable, and an unquenchable enthusiasm has provided the driving force. Work does not kill!

There has been no five-day week for me. I believe in work in large doses, undeterred by the brake which to-day is placed upon individual effort by our present system of crushing taxation. Money to me is not a prime reward. The success which has attended my efforts and the knowledge that the work has been appreciated by tens of thousands of readers all over the world has acted as a spur and provided a reward in itself.

I mentally visualise from my office the hundreds of thousands of readers depending upon my journals for help and guidance, and a strong sense of duty is within me to serve them. Fortunately I have been able to meet many thousands of them at exhibitions, at my lectures, and when visiting local clubs. I have found discussions with readers of great value in deciding what material to publish.

I mention these facts because in the hundreds of congratulatory letters I receive from readers and from leading members of the trade many have expressed astonishment that so much could have emanated from one man. I do not employ ghosts. Work bearing my signature is my own.

Many also have expressed surprise that one man could write on so many subjects. I suffer the penalty of versatility. My interests have always been wide; I have been associated with so many developments behind the scenes and with most of the famous names in radio, television, engineering and aviation all my life. As an engineer by education and training, I have been in the fortunate position of being asked to witness highly technical demonstrations which would not be comprehended by the usual non-technical journalist.

It has been part of my job to write for the man who does not know, and to convert highly technical matters into simple language. I am told by readers that the success of my journals is due in the main to that gift.

In the space of 21 years I have founded not only PRACTICAL WIRELESS, but several journals in other technical fields—the *Practical Motorist*, *The Cyclist*, *Practical Mechanics*, *Practical Television* and *Practical Engineering*. During the same span of time I have produced over 80 books, most of which have run through several editions, and are still in print, many having been translated into many other languages.

My large output could not be achieved by handwriting alone. Most of it is dictated and is typed as I talk; some is taken down in shorthand, some recorded on tape or wire, and only a small proportion written by hand. The latter is mathematical matter which defies the grammalogues of Mr. Pitman and even the skill of my expert stenographers.

Elsewhere in this issue I have summarised the history of PRACTICAL WIRELESS and the large number

Practical Wireless **'My 21 years as an Editor, 1932-1953'**

April, 1950 PRACTICAL WIRELESS

Practical Wireless

18th YEAR OF ISSUE

EVERY MONTH.
VOL. XXVI. No. 525 APRIL, 1950
Editor F. J. CAMM

COMMENTS OF THE MONTH BY THE EDITOR

"PRACTICAL TELEVISION"—Our New Companion Journal

No. 1 OF "PRACTICAL TELEVISION" WILL BE PUBLISHED ON MARCH 24th

THE rapid and ever-increasing development of the science of television and the great expansion in the number of viewers due to the opening of the Sutton Coldfield station—the forerunner of a chain of stations which will cover the country—makes it impossible for us in the small Practical Television section in this journal to devote sufficient space to deal with the construction of television receivers, new developments, news of the industry, new apparatus and that interchange of opinion which is so vital to a new industry.

The Practical Television supplement to this journal therefore assumes a separate entity on March 24th when the first issue of *Practical Television* will appear. It will be similar in format and arrangement to PRACTICAL WIRELESS. It will be controlled by the same editor and it will give the same faithful and unremitting services to its readers as with other journals in our Practical group.

It will cost ninepence every month, but to secure a copy it is essential that you place an order with your newsagent now, for although paper rationing as far as periodicals are concerned was abolished on March 1st, that does not mean that periodicals will be in unlimited supply. Paper pulp may not be available for the mills to supply the extra demand for paper.

Practical Television is launched at a time when the whole British public is eager to learn more about the new science. Interest is not confined to the two present service areas, for the great success of the Sutton Coldfield Station has caused the B.B.C. to modify its plans, with the result that other stations will be erected more speedily than was at first thought.

At present the two stations cover a service area of about 5,000 square miles, but technical interest is nation-wide; and whilst, therefore, the new journal in its early days will on its constructional side appeal mainly to readers within those two areas, the other features will have an educational appeal covering the whole country.

Practical Television will not only tell readers how to build television receivers, but also how to operate them, how to remedy faults, how to choose a receiver.

For example, the first issue will contain the first of a series of articles by the editor on "Television Principles and Practice," an article on the construction of a television receiver, television news from England and abroad; a B.B.C. television engineer explains the television transmitting system; an up-to-the-minute news feature; a helpful criticism and causerie; news from the industry; details of new receivers and accessories; an article on projection television; a short history of television; television personalities; the television systems of other countries; a review of some commercial television receivers; servicing television receivers; correspondence; an explanation of the Emitron Camera; also ultra short waves, news from the clubs, correspondence. These are but a few of the features which will be contributed by authorities only. The services of some of the leaders in the various television fields have already been retained.

As with all our journals, it will be lavishly illustrated in half tone and line.

We take pride in the fact that *Practical Television* will be the first new journal to commence publication after paper rationing ceased, for it appears 24 days after.—F.J.C.

Editorial and Advertisement Offices:
"Practical Wireless," George Newnes, Ltd.,
Tower House, Southampton Street, Strand,
W.C.2. 'Phone: Temple Bar 4363.
Telegrams: Newnes, Rand, London.
Registered at the G.P.O. for transmission by Canadian Magazine Post.

The Editor will be pleased to consider articles of a practical nature suitable for publication in "Practical Wireless." Such articles should be written on one side of the paper only, and should contain the name and address of the sender. Whilst the Editor does not hold himself responsible for manuscripts, every effort will be made to return them if a stamped and addressed envelope is enclosed. All correspondence intended for the Editor should be addressed: The Editor, "Practical Wireless," George Newnes, Ltd., Tower House, Southampton Street, Strand, W.C.2.

Owing to the rapid progress in the design of wireless apparatus and to our efforts to keep our readers in touch with the latest developments, we give no warranty that apparatus described in our columns is not the subject of letters patent.

Copyright in all drawings, photographs and articles published in "Practical Wireless" is specifically reserved throughout the countries signatory to the Berne Convention and the U.S.A. Reproductions or imitations of any of these are therefore expressly forbidden. "Practical Wireless" incorporates "Amateur Wireless."

Issue No. 1. *Practical Television*

Much of this information appeared as a series of articles in *Practical Wireless* encouraging him – or her – to build a simple apparatus starting e.g. with a one valve medium waveband receiver, and progressing to multivalve sets and the theory and practice of transmitting.

In the early days of post war television, experimenters were able to build sets sometimes using ex-service valves. The advertisement pages of the journals contain lists of unused radio components, schedules of valves, and offers of cathode ray tubes, as well as kits to build your own set.

F.J. published his *Practical Television Receiver* with instructions for making an 18 valve receiver. These covered 18 pages in large format. But commercial designs were becoming easy to rent or buy, and complex monster D.I.Y. sets fell from favour. So progress was overtaking the D.I.Y. approach to television.

In the early days of post war T.V., perhaps only one BBC station was in operation but lower power stations covering small areas throughout the country soon followed. Building your own pre-amplifier helped to get reception in marginal areas, and directions were to be found in F.J.'s articles.

Holidays spoiled by bad weather were alleviated by sets in boarding houses and hotels but F.J. was scornful at one time of the poor maintenance such sets were given. Political party conferences were transmitted after 1954. Colour T.V. developed in the U.S.A. The price of 12½" sets dropped from £350 to £175 in one day he reported. F.J.'s remark about the first concerts from Marconi House had been that these were – in 1954 – something like a bridal dress – something old, something new, something borrowed – but nothing blue!

About this time he earned the title of "The Great National Teacher of Wireless and Television".

F.J. Camm and Radar

F.J. was appointed a Life Member of the Radar Association formed in 1946. There were rumours that F.J. had been concerned with radar during the 1939-1945 war, but until a Blackpool bookseller catalogued what he described as "A scoop purchase for anyone interested in the wartime development of radar", little was known. The item was priced at £175 "The Lot", and read as follows:

"Numerous letters and notes of Squadron Leader Frank Preston* who was involved in Radar development in WW2 and who subsequently wrote articles for *Practical Wireless* about Radar and Communications etc. This "Lot" comprises hand-written notes to and typewritten replies from *Practical Wireless* magazine signed by its editor F.J. Camm regarding future articles about Radar, etc. and their clearance with the Air Ministry as most of the Radar information was top secret. Contained are over 70 Air Ministry photographs of Radar equipment, aerials, radar installations fitted in bombers and fighters, radar workshops, radar fitted in Lancaster Bombers. Secret papers on "Jamming equipment". H2s's installations fitted in aircraft. Numerous Air Ministry drawings marked SECRET of Mandrel "Auto Keying devices". Plus many items of correspondence regarding radar and communications. Over 150 pages/photographs/ drawings, notes etc. Fair to Good. An ideal acquisition for a museum or collector or radar historian. THE LOT £175."

The above collection was clearly important, and necessary to this biography. I tried to buy – only to find that "a Dutchman" had already bought the lot. He proved to be a Mr Derk Rouwhorst of Delden, Netherlands, who generously sent me photocopies including some letters sent by F.J. and Preston's replies.

Mr Rouwhorst added that "many of the letters are written on the backs of prints of secret Ministry drawings". (Because of the war time paper shortage?)

He added that he would exchange material for "H2S papers and books". I found that for the first two years of the war R.A.F. Bomber Command had operated singly by dead reckoning over Germany, with varying success. Later "beams" were transmitted, but these had limited range and accuracy. A self contained system operated from within the aircraft was required, and eventually one known as the H2S was used, one success being the accurate bombing of Hamburg. Then an aeroplane was lost with the H2S equipment.

The importance of H2S was such that the attack on Port Stanley during the Falklands war of May 1982 had H2S equipment in the R.A.F. Vulcan bombers.

No material for exchange could be found – probably because of my inexperience in the matter – and Mr Rouwhorst kindly sent almost all the collection for £100. This has to be conserved and examined knowledgeably and is now held by the Royal Windsor Collection. It includes Ministry permission to quote from secret papers. The purchase was funded by the Royal Albert Institute Trust of Windsor.

F.J.'s Miscellaneous Publications

While most of his output concerned wireless, television, engineering, mathematics, aviation, models and motoring and diesels, he is known to have written several books that were "one-offs". There was his book on "The Adjustment and repair of watches" (1940) in which his "practical" work included tuning a "keyless open-face "Solvill" pocket watch for a Kew Certificate of the National Physical Laboratory. He gained an "A" certificate. This was awarded for watches that did not depart from a mean daily rate standard for various positions. His effort received praise in the trade papers, which refer to him as "a collector and lover of watches".

His article in 1942 for *Tit-Bits* related the history of the British watch industry which had been allowed to go to foreign competitors, so that there was a wartime shortage of clocks, watches and materials for repairing them. He noted that "jewels" cost only "four shillings and 6 pence (22½p) a gross, except for high quality rubies and sapphires "that cost two or three shillings each" (ten or fifteen pence).

The Preface of his book *Watches, Adjustment and Repair* is of interest:–

> *Watch design and construction has changed considerably during the past 50 years. The old verge, fusee, duplex, rack and pinion, full plate, and similar early styles of watches have gone. The cylinder watch formerly considered to be the ultimate has given way to the modern anchor or detached escarpment with double roller. Watches have got smaller particularly in ladies' models, as well as thinner.*
>
> *Many of the books which deal with watch repair are out-of-date in that they deal with the repair of watches which now exist only as heirlooms. The change in watch construction has invited the publication of an up-to-date book dealing with modern methods of repair, adjustment, and timing; and in this present book I have endeavoured to supply the need, and to include information on the adjustment of a watch for passing the Kew test. Whilst this volume chiefly deals with modern watches for which interchangeable parts are available, the practical information given applies equally to all types of watch, with the exception of the additional complicated mechanisms such as calendar, split seconds and repeater details. These additions to the train would require a special volume to themselves. The book is intended as a manual for all those interested in horology, professionally or otherwise. The book represents many years of practical experience with all types of watches. Regular articles on this subject appear in my monthly journal Practical Mechanics. The Advice Bureau run in connection with this paper undertakes to reply to readers' questions on this fascinating subject.*
>
> *I wish to express my thanks to the Waltham Watch Company for permission to use certain illustrations and material relating to their watches; to the National Physical Laboratory for supplying details of their tests; to Mr. V. W. Clarke and the Editor of The Watchmaker's Jeweller for facts and illustrations relating to Hallmarks; to the Science Museum for permission to use illustrations of early watches; and to the proprietors of Practical Mechanics for permission to use illustrations and articles which appeared in the columns of that journal.*

In 1951 he edited Norman Hunter's *Successful conjuring for Amateurs, Marvels of Modern Science* was published in 1935 "Very fully illustrated" with a revised edition in 1938. This led to a Writ (see "F.J. goes to Law").

Occasionally he would co-operate with other writers, as with H.W. Gilbert-Rolfe and D.C. Nicholas in the 1945/47 editions of *Newnes Plastics Annual*.

In the days of his *Hobbies* writings for Newnes, he produced *Practical Leather Work* – a one shilling (5p) book telling about the tools and materials as well as working details of leather work and other home hobbies such as rug making, painting on leather, batik dyeing, gesso decoration and bead work. It covered the complete field of instruction – and unusually, for an F.J. book, was regarded as particularly interesting to ladies!

He co-operated with John Barnard for articles on model aeroplanes and other subjects for *The Handy Boys' Book* c. 1925.

Consecutive volumes of the *Practical Mechanics* and others in the *Practical* series are very difficult to trace. Some of the most important public libraries only have part sets (e.g. Aberdeen, Birmingham, Shoreditch, St. Pancras, – and Chicago, also Sydney, Australia, and apparently the Science Museum Library. It has not been possible to make a comprehensive list, I suggest that some of the "Lottery Loot" should be used to remedy the situation!

It is clear from letters received from F.J. fans that there are odd examples and part sets held all over the country. Many of these are treasured by octogenarians and others, and it is to be hoped that they will not suffer the fate of George Camm's collection at Windsor, which was scattered by executors before action could be taken. The ROYAL WINDSOR COLLECTION is trying to collect his books and journals despite financial difficulties. (Dr. Judith Hunter, BSc, PhD, The Royal Borough Collection, 26 Wood Lane, Slough, SL1 9EA). The collection is aided by THE FRIENDS OF THE ROYAL BOROUGH COLLECTION. Dr. Hunter is a part-time Honorary Curator at the Royal Borough of Windsor & Maidenhead Store, Tinkers Lane, Windsor.

F.J.'s Coterie

A coterie of experts surrounded F.J. There was his wireless sub-editor, W.J. Delaney, H.J. Barton Chapple, Wh.Sch, BSc (Hons), A.C.G.I., A.M.I.E.E., W.B. Richardson and Frank Preston F.R.A. who was F.J.'s assistant for many years. He became (1942) Squadron Leader Preston, and based at High Wycombe he corresponded with F.J. towards the end of the war on several subjects – including resuming his old job, and radar.

Writers of reviews for his publications sometimes recalled working with F.J. as did the *Morning Advertiser* motoring correspondent in November 1939, concerning a timely article on "More Miles Per Gallon" about fuel economy measures "for every make of car, and the use of alternative fuels".

His wide scope embraced model aviation, electrical engineering – especially wireless – and mechanical engineering, also horology and general model making as well as the "Cambro" three wheeler and two other cars. His gift for drawing diagrams of circuits and layouts, each of such clarity that they were readily understood, was known from his school days.

He conveyed his enthusiasm for his many and varied subjects to his students, for whom he wrote as well as for their teachers, resulted in his being hailed as "That great national teacher, F.J. Camm, the author of many standard works on radio, television and mechanical engineering".

F.J.'s Pseudonyms (and obsessions)

An early one was "Waysider" used in his *Book of the New Imperial* motor cycle for Pitman. One that he used every month in *Practical Wireless* on a popular page entitled "On your Wavelength" was "Thermion". He admitted that sometimes he received letters from readers who disagreed with his views, complaining that "I hide behind a nom-de-plume" (January 1956 – when he justified his course at length). "Thermion" claimed to be the "first radio journalist over 37 years".

The thoughts behind the paragraphs under the "Thermion" heading help to reveal F.J.'s character and even his obsessions. He approved the BBC religious programmes, "they are conducted in accord with the tenents of Christian teaching".

Those who challenged his views – including W. Graham who he challenged to a public debate – a challenge that was not accepted – found that he "could find a biblical quotation which cancelled out the revivalists who quoted the Bible at me".

He was proud of being one of the few original exhibitors at the Radio Show "who had been present at each of the entire run of shows from 1923 to 1956". Another bee in his bonnet was "Jamming", especially on the short wave bands, from transmitters – mostly in Russia but also in Poland "and other subjugated countries" – who considered the Voice of America and the BBC to be "slanderous and an insult to their dignity". F.J. noted that the British Government once jammed broadcasts of Radio Athens and the Egyptian Broadcasting Service (November 1956). He noted the need for car radios and really portable miniature radio sets, both were very rare in those days of 1930. *Practical Wireless* included layouts for these sets. He disagreed with electronic organs, "Mrs Dale's Diary", "Life with the Lyons" "which should be rested" but was interested in history about wireless, from the first wireless life saving at sea (3rd March 1899) onwards: also aeronautical history.

"Letters after names" by reason of payment of an annual subscription without a qualifying examination were objected to – he made a practice as sub-editor of deleting from an author's name all but registered degrees. He was an R.S.A. fellow from 1936 until his death. Some of his pseudonyms were "Waysider" (Cycling & Motorcycling), "Thermion" (Wireless), "Jay Cee" (Models), "Haycraft" (Motor cycles), "Frederick Jace" (Wood turning). Articles were sometimes signed F.J.C.

F.J.'s Patents

F.J. designed and patented at least three things, including a "New or Improved Collapsible Punt or Pontoon Number 534,309 (Application 20th December 1939, 32564/39). He also patented "Improvements in or relating to Pyrophoric Lighters" Number 581,286. (Application 22nd August 1944, accepted 8th October 1946). This is stated to "overcome any problem due to the wick being consumed, or a fresh flint becoming necessary". A number of these were manufactured. One is in the Windsor collection.

His patent for an "Improved Method of and Means for Inflating Pneumatic Tyres of Road Vehicles" (generally a cycle) was worked off a road wheel, and inflated the tyre as this turned. This was approved in November 1945 – and F.J. demonstrated his invention on T.V. in December 1946. A photograph duly appeared in *Practical Wireless*. (Patent 587,861, No. 1887/45).

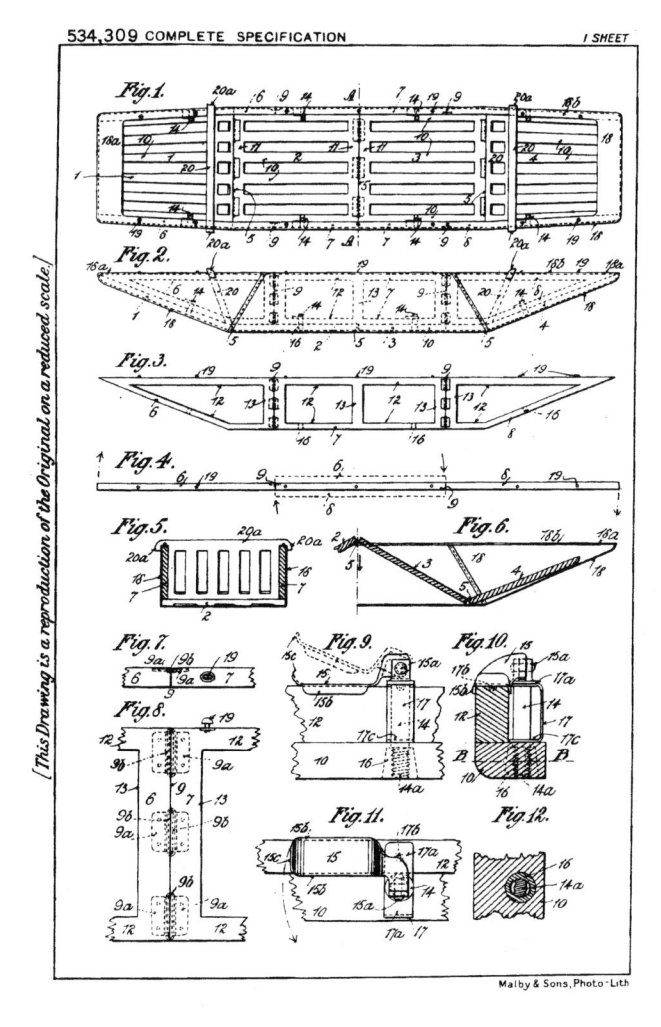

A new or Improved Collapsible Pont or Pontoon

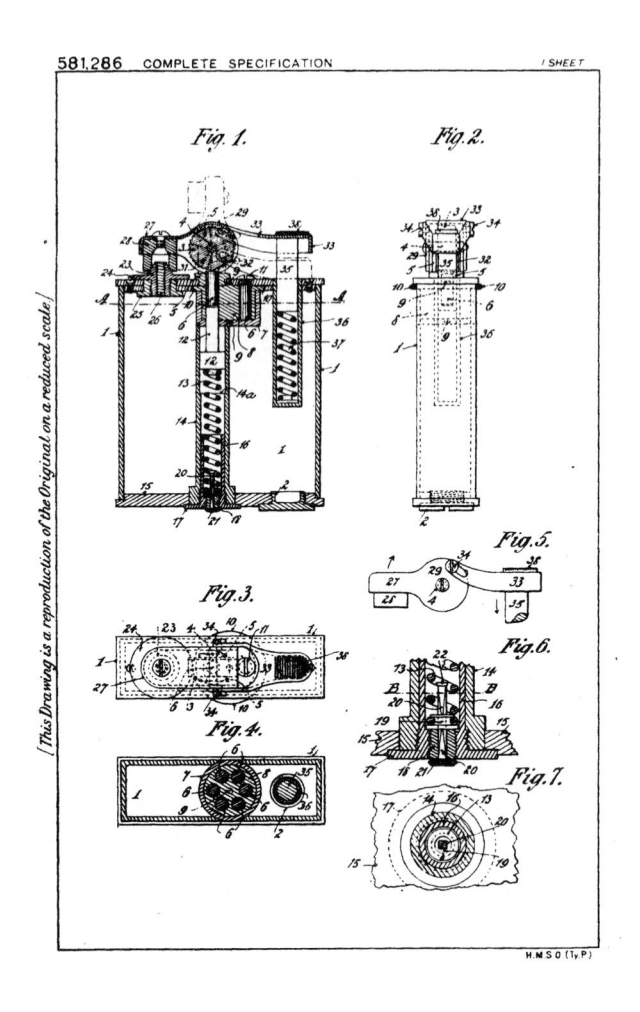

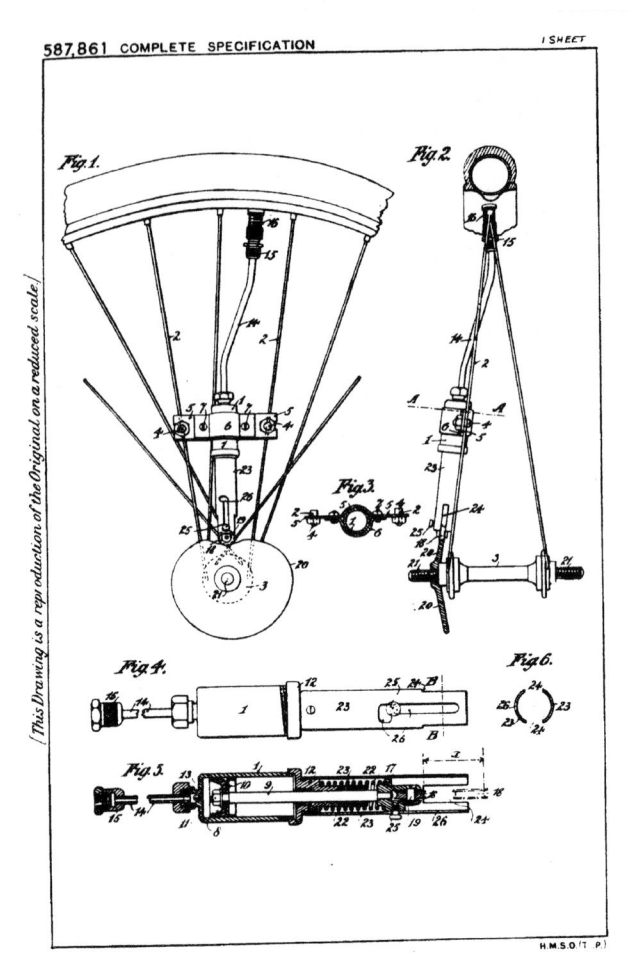

Phosphoric Lighter **Pneumatic Tyre Inflator**

F.J. The "Eminent Wartime Journalist"

He supported the exhortation of the then Minister of Supply, Mr Herbert Morrison, to all armament workers that "If we waste a minute at our bench or desk we sacrifice a life" ... He used this to criticise the mobile police who summoned munitions workers who exceeded the speed limit when hastening to work because the consequential delays might result in losing an hour's production.

He also criticised aircraft factory managers who ordered workers to go to the shelters whenever the siren sounded. This resulted in local warning schemes whereby observers rang bells or gave other warnings when VI flying bombs approached. This was arranged in some factories west of London which tended to be beyond the normal V1 range, and were expected to drop short.

He added that workers who did overtime six or seven days a week expected to find transport home, but sometimes they were stranded because buses, trams and trains had ceased to run – the very effect that Hitler wanted – to disorganise industry and communications.

As the Editor of important technical journals and a writer of technical books in great demand, his opinions were sought, as by the *World's Press News* dated 28th May 1942.

Less Spectacular Journalism

By F. J. CAMM, Editor of "Practical Engineering," etc.

THE trade and technical Press of this country represents the less spectacular side of journalism, but the Government is alert to the highly important part it is playing in the war. Standardisation and mass-production created the days of specialism, and thereby the specialist journal. Whereas formerly technical journals were of the portmanteau type, covering a wide variety of diverse subjects and industries, to-day journals cover one industry and its cognate industries.

Thus, the technical Press filters the public and industries according to their respective interests, and advertisers as well as Government departments are able to make a more direct approach to particular interests.

The work performed by the technical journals is not always appreciated, although Ministries have paid tribute to the way in which the technical Press is performing its important war-time job amid difficult conditions of paper supply and staff shortage. Its work is an essential part of the drive for higher production, and it is an essential industry in itself.

Saving Time and Trouble

Technical journals, as was admitted recently, stage a conference of the industries they serve once a week or once a month as the case may be. They bring news of the latest results of research and the practical application of new production ideas. Experts in particular subjects give their knowledge to the whole of industry. Technical journals abstract the essential points and save industry an immense amount of time and trouble.

The advertisements provide valuable technical information for firms engaged on war work. The journals thus save the time which would otherwise be spent in experiment.

Editorial criticisms often save manufacturers from disaster; they indicate the flaws in a policy or a product and conversely, because of the knowledge which the editor of a technical journal must have of the tendency in the whole of a particular industry (for he is in touch with all firms), he quite often is able to guide manufacturers on to new production lines.

The Technical Journalist

The technical journalist does not subscribe to the old Fleet Street doctrine that a good journalist can write on any subject. A technical journalist has to be doubly skilled; he must be a good journalist in the first place and a responsible one, and he must also possess a first-class technical education and have workshop experience in a large number of subjects and in a large number of industries, especially that which his journal serves.

He must understand trade agreements, trade policies, Board of Trade requirements, the important sources of information; he must attend important trade meetings and lectures, inspect new inventions, visit factories, and he must give a prompt service to his readers so that he keeps abreast of his competitors. He must fearlessly expose trade rackets.

Press Supports Its Trade

It is often thought that the trade "supports" its Press. It is more accurate to say that the Press supports the industries it represents, for in many cases (wireless is a good example) the Press created industries.

This country was fortunate when it went to war in having available such a large number of specialist journals, each of which immediately switched over to the war effort. The Services have absorbed into important executive positions many of the skilled staffs of the trade Press. My own staff, many of whom have distinguished themselves in this war are performing good work. My own journals have made useful contributions to the war effort, not only by indicating new process of manufacture to speed up production, by indicating alternative materials and methods of manufacture, by advising Government departments on special problems, by finding personnel, and by other work of an extremely confidential character, but also by producing instruction manuals and reference books, which I know have been of immense value.

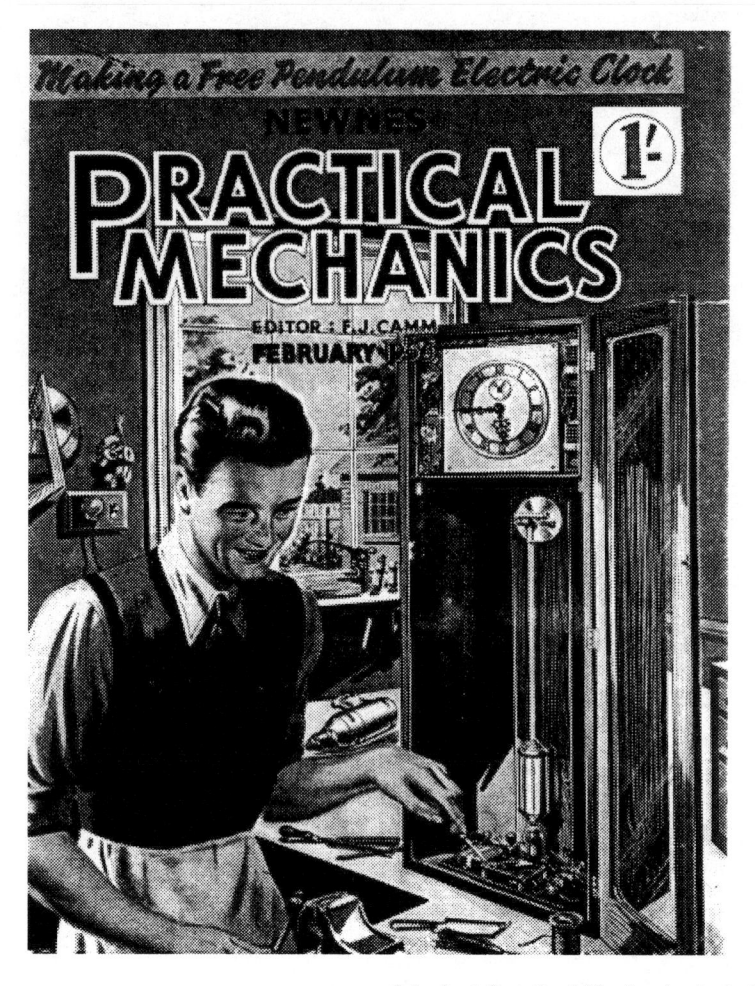

A typical *Practical Mechanics* jacket

F.J. Camm and "Practical Mechanics' " Silver Jubilee

This section presented problems, by reason of the success of F.J.'s original object that "the Editorial policy should be on the widest possible lines, covering science, invention, mechanics, model making and all of the wide variety of practical subjects".

His sources were world wide, and the field infinitely broad. This journal embodied others in the *Practical* series and so aeroplane models are described in *Hobbies*, and radios are to be found as well as in the specialist *Practical Wireless*, which flourished from a start a year earlier in 1932. As well as his motoring and motor cycle books – with the *Practical Motoring Encyclopaedia* of 1935 – the same year as his *Home Mechanics Encyclopaedia* – there were what may be termed "thematic" publications which he listed on the title page of such publications as his *Practical Mechanics Handbook* (1938) and in the comprehensive *Newnes Engineer's Reference Book* with its long history of revised editions after the first publication in 1946. The latter plus 2,000 pages of truly enormous comprehensive effort collected information and references previously scattered among several volumes. There were revised editions almost every year, as former standards were abolished and modern fresh standards substituted. Not that old standards were omitted – where these remained in use, F.J. ensured that they continued to be included.

The previous *Workshop Handbooks* each contained information of value to only a few. The comprehensive *Practical Mechanics Handbook* included "Facts, Figures, Table and Formulae for the Mechanic, Fitter, Turner, Draughtsman, and Engineer" with hundreds of illustrations and the meticulous index that F.J. provided.

F.J. was fascinated with the possibilities and methods of operation of "The Mechanical Man" and Robots, and published a review in *Practical Mechanics* in October 1958. These anticipations of the "Animotronics" of Disneyland of recent years (but not cybernetics and other technical terms not yet in the dictionaries) were mentioned by F.J.

I am very grateful to all the *Practical Mechanics* "fans" who have drawn my attention to such examples in their collections. It is sad that within a year F.J. was to die, and the April 1959 *Practical Mechanic* contains an obituary, as did the other journals in Newnes *Practical* series.

F.J.'s +117 publications excluding the periodicals are listed in the end of this biography. Even this list is not comprehensive.

It is not easy to find complete volumes of *Practical* journals for reference, and I trust that owners will arrange for their treasured volumes to be made available in public libraries and/or the Royal Windsor Collection which has a F.J. CAMM section for which donations of his books and journals are most welcome.

Our Silver Jubilee and the Three Wheel £20 Car

In October 1958 F.J. reviewed 25 years of continuous publication of Newnes *Practical Mechanics*, and this is included verbatim.

The review mentions "Our £20 Car". This was a three wheel single seat car. A description, dated April 1936 follows.

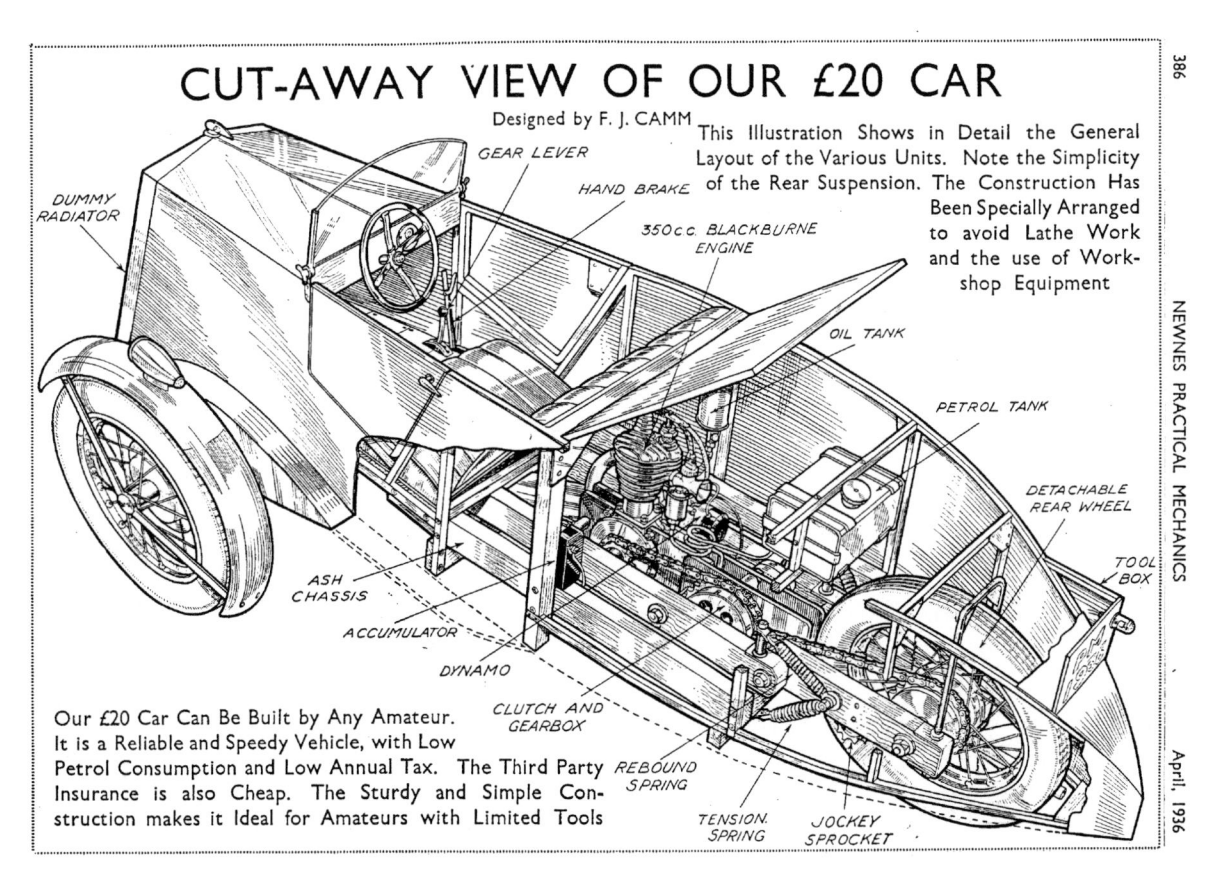

Cut-away View of the £20 3-Wheeled Car

NEWNES PRACTICAL MECHANICS — October, 1958

Our Silver Jubilee

A Review of Our 25 Years of Continuous Publication
By the Editor

THIS issue of PRACTICAL MECHANICS celebrates 25 years of continuous publication—its Silver Jubilee. It was the second of our Practical Group of journals to have attained 25 years of continuous publication, with only one break due to the printing strike. For it was in 1933 that, following the success of *Practical Wireless*, that it was decided to launch PRACTICAL MECHANICS. Its editorial policy was based on the widest possible lines. It was planned to cover the spheres of science, invention, mechanics, model making and all of the wide range of practical subjects. It was evident in 1933 that new sciences and new techniques had brought about a change in pubic interests. They were looking for something more modern and of wider vision than the craft magazines of the period, which were chiefly concerned with model making.

The Launch

Therefore PRACTICAL MECHANICS was launched in October, 1933, at a time when the scientific world was undergoing a rapid metamorphosis. Television was on the way, nuclear energy was dawning, aircraft were beginning to take on a new form, both as to higher speeds and engine design, the plastic industry was beginning to branch out, space flight was being considered as a possibility in the near future, the motor car had taken on a new form, the diesel engine was getting under way, electronic engineering had established itself as a new industry, high speed ocean-going liners were replacing the ships of older type and new industries, founded on new sciences, were springing up almost every month.

A strong feature of this journal has always been its practical constructional articles. Here are sketches of the P.M. Trailer Caravan and Catamaran

News From All Quarters!

It has been a most fascinating quarter of a century and we made it our policy to bring to our readers month by month the latest information of developments in all these directions gathered from the four quarters of the globe. In many cases, readers first learned of these developments from the pages of this journal, often months ahead of the daily press and technical journals. The hobby-minded public were turning from model locomotives and from ornamental turning and other practical crafts to power-driven model aircraft, full-size gliders and light aeroplanes.

Scoops

This journal, therefore, dealt with the construction of the Flying Flea, the Luton Minor light monoplane, full-size gliders, power-driven model aircraft and radio-control of models to satisfy the increasing interest in these newer hobbies. We set a new standard in journalism, not only by the broadness of the editorial field, but also with the exceptional reader service we gave through our Free Advisory Service. We specialised in a wealth of illustrations and it can fairly be said that we set a pattern which many other publishers have endeavoured without success to emulate. *Practical Wireless*, when this journal came out, was two years old and in that period its great success had caused all its competitors except one to fall by the wayside.

Unique

The first issue of PRACTICAL MECHANICS rapidly sold out and, month by month, orders for it increased until they reached its present very high level. PRACTICAL MECHANICS remains the only journal of its type in this country and it is very pleasant to be able to record that many thousands of those who took the first issue are still readers to-day.

Hundreds of readers paid generous tribute to the part this journal has played in earning them promotion. Many, ideed, call at these offices to record their appreciation in person. Technical schools and colleges soon found that it was a journal their scholars should read, as it provided an auxiliary education and stimulated interest in the subjects included in the school curriculum. PRACTICAL MECHANICS is on the approved list of the London County Council and most other educational authorities throughout the country.

Inventors in hundreds have appealed to us for advice, and in a large number of cases we have helped them on the road to success and in an even larger number have saved them from the financial disaster which follows when over-enthusiasm for the possibilities of an invention has blinded them to the commercial drawbacks.

Attack by the Conjurors

It has not always been easy to carry out such a bold editorial policy, for trade associations in some cases resented our exposure of what had hitherto been considered as trade secrets. For example, when we launched our series of articles giving details of conjuring tricks, a magicians' union threatened action against us for what they considered to be "infringement of copyright" in their tricks. A fund was raised through

The practical policy extended from full-size to model. We were early in the field with a design for a model powered racing car and power-driven aircraft and boats. But equally we gave practical experiments in chemistry and electricity.

the pages of an entertainment journal in order to prosecute the writ. After the conjurors had taken counsel's opinion, they learned what they should have known, that there is no copyright in a trick as such and their greatest illusion was that they ever had a case at all. The writs were, of course, withdrawn and our reply to the threat was more articles exposing the secrets of conjuring.

The conjurors, I believe, subscribed quite generously to this fighting fund, but I never discovered what happened to the money so raised. The conjurors had for many years been extorting money from other publishers in this way, publishers who preferred to pay rather than fight.

To protect them from future attacks by conjurors we reported the facts to *World's Press News* and other trade papers. One paper humorously commented that whilst we were naturally jubilant with our victories over the rabbit out of a hat merchants, we should be careful that someone did not arrive outside Tower House with a small conjuring table, utter a few words of conjurors' mumbo-jumbo and transport George Newnes, Ltd., and myself, to the Gobi Desert!

There was a diversity of topics; the above sketch is a reminder that we described how to build garages and how to spray the car. The bottom sketch shows our full-sized hydroplane.

Our £20 Car

Soon after this journal was launched I considered that a small runabout car which readers could build for themselves was wanted by a large public which could not afford to buy the cheapest car then on the market. Accordingly, I spent the evenings and weekends over a period of some months designing and building such a car.

It was not designed around pieces of old motor cars obtained from the breaker's yard but from new components available for all from stockists. It could be built for just over £20 and it was called the "£20 Car." Many hundreds of them have been built since then. It complied in every particular with the Road Vehicles Construction and Use Orders which is more perhaps than can be said for some of the designs now being published, which are built round breaker's yard components, and which do not comply with the law. In any case some will have to be submitted to the 10-year-old test.

The Flying Flea

The Frenchman, M. Mignet, at that time under the sponsorship of a daily newspaper, had created national interest in his little miniature aeroplane the Pou de Ciel, or the Flying Louse, but which we in this country rechristened the Flying Flea. This journal, alone of the technical press of this country, made arrangements with him to publish full working drawings of the machine and clubs were started all over the country to build it from those designs. Although a large number were built and successfully flown, there is no record of any of them suffering an accident.

Boats

From cars and aeroplanes to boats was a natural transition and, apart from rowing and sailing boats, we published designs for cabin cruisers, outboard motor boats, and other powered craft. This was the first journal to publish constructional details for a television receiver, which at that time, of course, was a disc machine of the Baird pattern designed for the low-definition (30 line) transmissions of the period. High-definition came much later.

Space Travel

In the 30's too, the Interplanetary Society had been founded by a group of enthusiasts who believed in the possibilities of space flight, and accordingly we commissioned one of the leaders of the movement to write a series of articles on the subject dealing with past experiments, history and present and future developments. Other journals pooh-poohed the idea of space flight. I, however, took the view that space flight was possible, and that it was only a matter of time and money to achieve interplanetary travel. It must be a source of gratification to those early space enthusiasts, as it is indeed a tribute to the pre-vision we showed, to see the fulfilment in part of their dreams, as exemplified by the Russian and American artificial satellites which have successfully demonstrated the theories put forth 25 years ago by the Interplanetary Society.

Interspersed with scientific articles typified by the foregoing, we regularly published articles on model making, chemistry, radio, electronics, lathe work, photography, cinematography, and matter which is now known under the general label of D.I.Y.

Our Companion Journals

The great success of these two journals caused us to turn our minds to an expansionist policy of producing practical journals in other spheres, and the next journal on the list was the *Practical Motorist*, which was published pre-war as a weekly, was suspended during the war and reappeared four years ago as a monthly publication. It quickly achieved a larger circulation than any other motoring periodical and it has become the leader in this field. Very naturally other publishers, impressed by the great success of our journals, endeavoured to jump on the bandwagon, but unsuccessfully. Some did not last a couple of years.

Shortly after the *Practical Motorist* came *The Cyclist*. This became one of the early casualties during the war and has become a supplement to this journal.

There followed *Practical Television*, launched just after the Television Advisory Committee had issued its report in favour of the television service. This, however, was ahead of its time, so publication was suspended when the war started, but it has since reappeared and it remains alone as the only practical publication dealing with television in this country. Like PRACTICAL MECHANICS, it is essentially practical and has published several designs for home-built television receivers.

We regularly published articles on the practical crafts such as lathe work and the use of hand tools in wood and metal.

The Practical Householder

But the greatest triumph was yet to come. Just after the war householders began to take a keener interest in house decoration and repair. Special power tools, prints, and materials were being produced and it was obvious from our query service that we could not hope to deal in this journal with all of the D.I.Y. subjects in demand. Accordingly, we launched *The Practical Householder* which immediately achieved an enormous circulation approaching the million mark (it twice exceeded it) and which in spite of journals started in competition with it maintains its lead by hundreds of thousands over all of them.

The great success which has attended the Practical Group of periodicals is a source of satisfaction to all those associated with it and we gratefully acknowledge the loyalty of our vast band of readers who have gathered round our banner and made this possible.

CONGRATULATIONS
A Few of the Hundreds of Birthday Greetings We Have Received

From LORD BRABAZON OF TARA

Many congratulations on 25 years' publication of PRACTICAL MECHANICS. This paper has given tremendous pleasure to thousands of people in every home, and I sincerely hope it will long continue its useful work.

From R. A. FULLER
(Joint Managing Director Bassett-Lowke, Ltd.)

Mr. Whynne (W. J.) Bassett-Lowke would have particularly enjoyed writing this letter for he knew and admired the enthusiasm and industry which launched PRACTICAL MECHANICS.

At that difficult period it was a courageous adventure which rapidly reaped the reward of a steadily increasing readership. The policy of dealing with a wide variety of subjects and keeping readers informed of technical and scientific developments in good, readable English well justified the choice of its name.

Right from those early days we have advertised in your columns and continue to do so for the best of reasons —it's good business.

Congratulations on reaching the 25th Anniversary of PRACTICAL MECHANICS. It is a grand record of past achievement with a great prospect for future development.

From A. H. WHITELEY, M.B.E
(Founder and Managing Director Whiteley Electrical Co. Ltd.)

It is with much pleasure that I send congratulations to PRACTICAL MECHANICS on its fine record. From the early pioneering days the magazine has encouraged a practical interest in mechanical construction and design. Under the inspired direction of its founder-editor, F. J. Camm, intricate and complicated technical details have been presented to its readers in simple, easy to grasp language, so that enthusiastic amateurs in all parts of the world have been able to enjoy the fruits of mechanical development and, often, to play a part in the progress.

I trust that the good work of PRACTICAL MECHANICS may be continued for many years so that readers may keep pace with the long and rapid strides we are witnessing in the field of modern mechanics.

From F. H. BARNES
(Publicity Manager the Telegraph Condenser Co. Ltd.)

Twenty-five years is a memorable milestone in the life of any publication, particularly when its appeal is only to a specialised readership, and I am therefore very pleased to send my congratulations to PRACTICAL MECHANICS.

In so doing, I fully realise that the congratulations and good wishes are primarily to Mr. F. J. Camm. Even his optimism could not have foreseen that the fledgeling he launched in 1933 would, a quarter of a century later, enjoy such a phenomenal circulation.

We were in from the beginning, for a T.C.C. advertisement appeared in the first issue. In remembering this, may I sincerely hope that in another 25 years "P.M." will be equally—if not more—popular with another generation of enthusiasts.

From BURNE-JONES & CO. LTD.

From the advanced age of 38 years and as the second electronic and radio company to be established in Great Britain, being preceded only by Marconi, Burne-Jones & Co. Ltd. take great pleasure in offering their heartiest congratulations to PRACTICAL MECHANICS on attaining their 25th birthday.

A quarter of a century ago we advertised in the first issue of this journal offering a dual gang condenser for an early type radio. To-day we specialise in high fidelity sound equipment. In all the years that have seen rapid development in radio, television and sound reproduction, we have found the columns of PRACTICAL MECHANICS helpful and stimulating and its advertising space fruitful.

PRACTICAL MECHANICS are to be complimented on their pioneer work in this field and we look forward to a continued friendly association with this journal and its readers and wish it Many Happy Returns.

The Four Wheeled Midget car of May 1937

Following the Three Wheel Car of 1936 came the Four Wheel Midget Car of 1937. This was the result of readers asking how to widen the body of the three wheeler to take a passenger.

F.J. advised against modification, and produced a two seater in May 1937. The engine was to be 500 – 750 c.c., single or twin cylinder with a three speed motor cycle gear box, having a top gear ratio of 7 to 1. Air cooling of the engine was to be assisted by a blast of air from under the moving car, direct on to the cylinder block.

There was no differential to the back axle, as "I have not deemed it necessary". He pointed out that the "Bleriot Whippet light car of a few years earlier had no differential". (It is true that a differential gear can be dispensed with altogether without serious consequences and with only occasional inconvenience. With a solid axle one wheel will slip on curves).

He added that standard ¼-elliptic springs can be picked up cheaply at car breakers.

The three wheel cars had the advantage that as the official designation is that it is a motor cycle, it was not necessary for a qualified driver to accompany the beginner, apart from fitting the "L" plate if a motor cycle licence was not held prior to April 1934. Even a third party insurance policy cost only £3. 7 shillings and 6d (£3.37½p). The make was to be registered as CAMM. (His own registration number was CXR 547 – "Stop me on the road if you wish to ask any questions".)

Blue prints were offered for ten shillings and 6d a set (52p) for several years until about 1950, with free constructional details.

April, 1936   NEWNES PRACTICAL MECHANICS   387

BUILDING OUR £20 CAR

The First Article on the construction of this ingenious three-wheeler appeared last month. Many hundreds of readers have already commenced construction and we have received an enormous amount of correspondence. As stated last month this car can be built for even less than £20, its annual tax is only £4, and it is capable of 50 miles an hour. It may be driven by any reader over 16 years of age, and its petrol consumption is over 65 miles per gallon. Best of all, it may be built by any amateur, for the construction has been simplified to avoid skilled fitting, turning, and brazing. A further article will appear next month.

By F. J. Camm

I COMMENCE this month by disposing of some queries I have received. As these queries are of a general character, I shall thus arrest the pen of other correspondents who may wish to ask similar queries.

Firstly, regarding the blue prints. These will be ready in a fortnight's time and will cost 10s. 6d. the set of four sheets. This may seem rather a lot of money, but they are being produced for the convenience of readers and the work entailed in their preparation is heavy. It will also be appreciated that the demand for them will be comparatively small, and it is impossible therefore to produce them cheaper.

Those readers who wish to proceed with the construction in advance of the publication of further details will, if they purchase a set of blue prints, be enabled to do so. Which brings me to another question which I have received from many readers. I cannot send drawings and details through the post in advance of publication. The preparation of separate drawings and sketches and descriptions involves, unfortunately, more time than I have to spare, and queries should be confined to materials, choice of engine's, gearboxes, etc.

Conversion to a Two-seater

As I anticipated, I have received shoals of letters from those who wish to convert the design into a two-seater. This I do not advise, nor do I think that anyone can reasonably expect to build a passenger-carrying vehicle for £20.

This car has been designed as a monocar, and one must draw the line somewhere. Suppose, for example, I altered the design so that it could be used as a passenger-carrying vehicle; this would mean that the whole structure would need to be strengthened, would be considerably heavier, require a more powerful engine, involve a higher insurance premium, need a heavier gearbox, and so on. Moreover, it would invite queries as to how the design could be amended to carry a third passenger, and even a fourth. Those readers who are minded to do so, can easily adapt the designs here given. I had in mind when producing the designs for this car a vehicle as speedy as a motor cycle, but with the added advantages of weather protection. I also had in mind economy of construction and low running costs, and set myself the limit of £20. Deviation from this along the lines which so many readers have been kind enough to suggest would bring the cost of materials alone up to £30 or £40, and for this figure you can pur-

The £20 Car!

Building our £20 Car

The Albion gearbox.

chase an excellent second-hand three- or four-wheeled car.

The Engine

And now regarding engines. Readers apparently have experienced no difficulty in obtaining offers of second-hand motor-cycle engines and gearboxes at prices varying from 20s. to 30s. The engine which I have selected is the 350-c.c. side-valve Blackburne, and I am using the well-known Albion gearbox, to the manufacturers of both of which I desire to tender my thanks for their co-operation in placing units at my disposal. An engine which is eminently suitable for this car is the unit-constructed New Imperial engine which also has the gearbox incorporated. Thus, in the one-unit you save yourselves the trouble of having to make two mounting plates—if you can call simple metal-work a troublesome operation. It isn't really.

Another question which has produced a volume of correspondence is that concerning the steering system. I show herewith photographs of the type of steering which I have used. This is similar to that which was fitted on the Carden car, a popular light car which was on the market a few years ago. The great advantage of this system is that it dispenses with leaf-springs, which are somewhat expensive. It will be seen that the steering heads are mounted between the springs, which in themselves absorb the road shocks; no other form of additional front suspension is necessary.

Type of Steering

A further advantage of this type of steering is that it eliminates the need for a geared steering box such as would be necessary on a heavier car, but quite unnecessary on a light vehicle of this description. Thus, it will be appreciated that direct steering is employed. It is easy to make, and satisfactory in every way. The front axle merely consists of two pieces of angle iron which can be purchased locally, and which are bolted direct to the chassis members. Nothing could be much simpler than that. I shall give detailed drawings, of course, so that the reader can make up the steering system himself, although he will need to purchase the hubs and rims. Complete wheels will be supplied by the British Hub Company, whose address readers may have on application. It will be seen that the internal expanding brakes are incorporated in the hubs. If you are skilled at wheel building (I shall give instructions on how to assemble and true the wheels) the cost is very low. I have made arrangements with a manufacturer to supply the steering heads to our readers for a nominal sum, although, of course, they can be cut from the solid if it is desired to save even that expense.

But it is not essential that the type of steering illustrated should be used; you may use, for example, the front axle assembly of an Austin "7," provided that you are able to purchase also the steering box, and the semi-elliptic front springs. These are quite easily mounted by

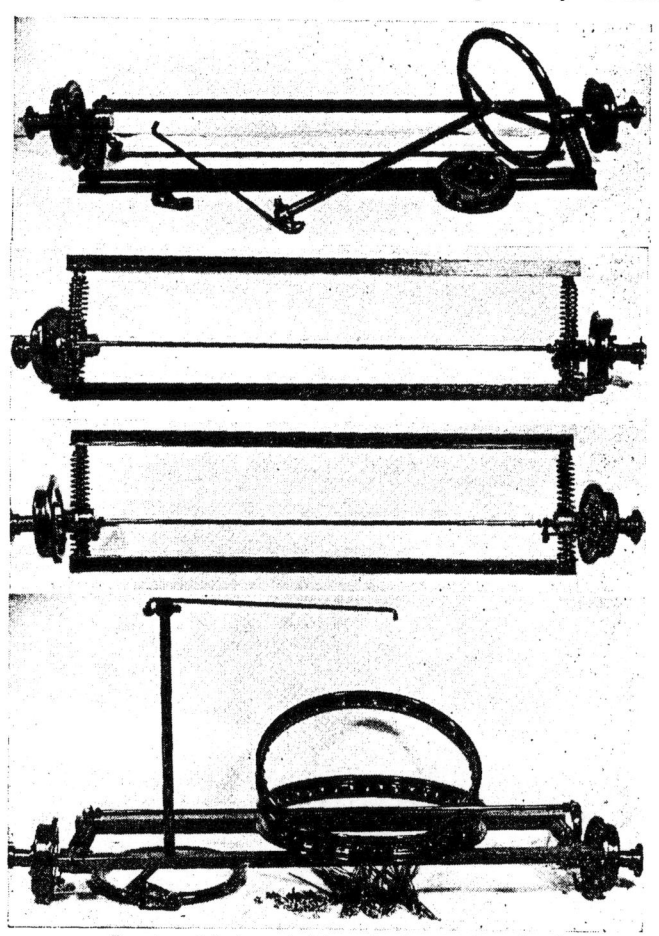

Four views of the front axle, hubs, track rod, rims, spokes, and nipples.

Building our £20 Car

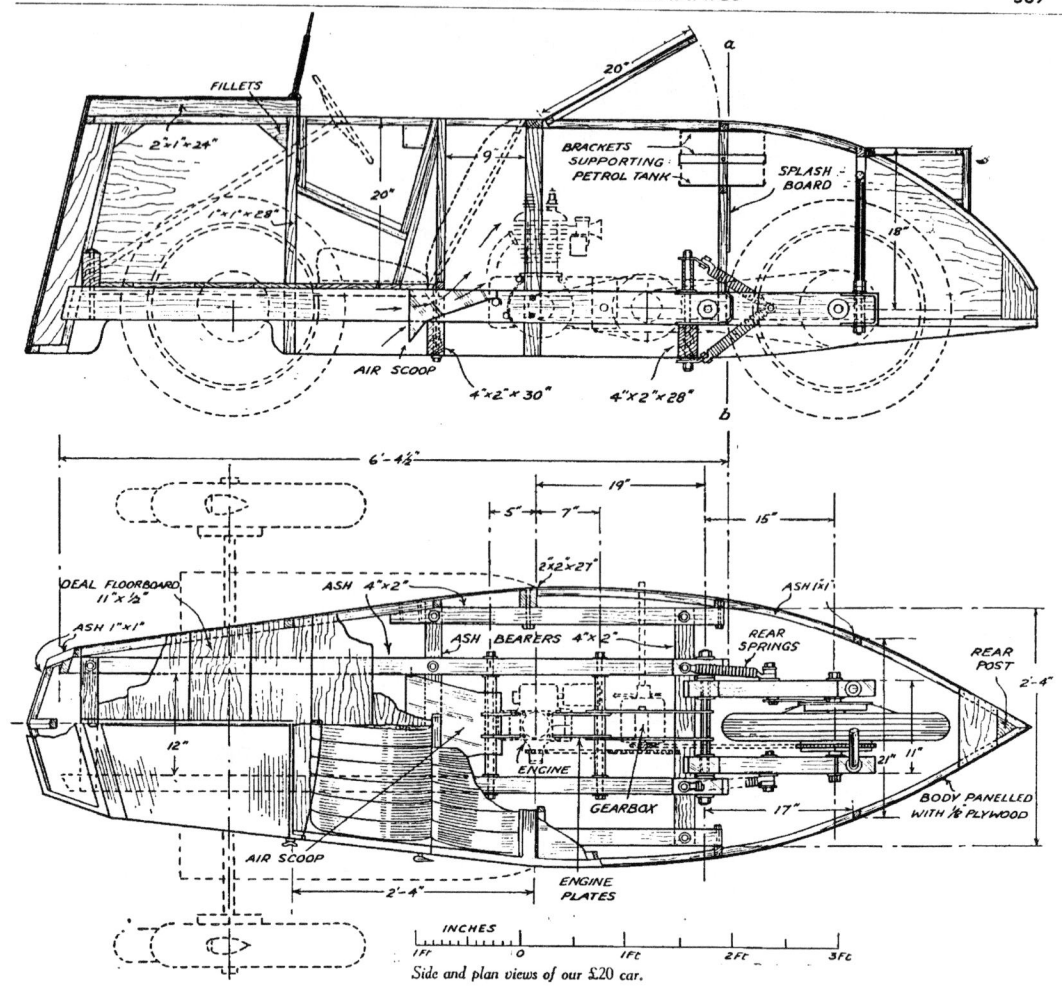

Side and plan views of our £20 car.

means of the shackles, as on the Austin "7." It is possible to pick up a complete front axle and assembly quite cheaply from the car breakers.

The Rear Wheel

For the rear wheel I have selected one of the quickly detachable wheels with knock-through spindle as fitted to the Norton and Rudge-Whitworth motor cycles; thus, in the case of a puncture in the rear tyre, the rear wheel can easily be removed by uncoupling the rear chain and knocking out the spindle. The rear members which carry the front wheel are made of wood; if you are a skilled metal-worker you will, of course, braze up a pair of rear forks. But wood is quite satisfactory, and easy to work. I am aware that some of the methods employed in this car are not those used by car manufacturers, but I have had in mind all the time the amateur who has only a few tools. The methods I have employed I have found from experience to be quite satisfactory.

For the rear suspension I have used tension springs. These can be purchased locally, and springs of the type used in the front forks of motor cycles will suit. It will be noted that as the rear members are not pivoted on a centre coinciding with the centre of the gearbox sprocket, a jockey sprocket must be fitted to compensate for the varying chain tensions.

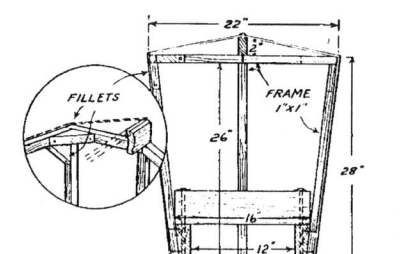

The frame of the dummy radiator viewed from the rear.

List of Materials

Several readers have asked for a list of materials, but it is obviously not possible to give this in complete form because each reader will be using a different make of engine and gearbox. The drawings given this month, however, will enable each

Building our £20 Car

reader to get together the necessary components. If you have not yet commenced construction, the first thing to do is to get together an engine, gearbox, three wheels, and the front axle. From these components you can erect the chassis, leaving the superstructure until last. The chassis consists of 4 in. × 2 in. ash bearers, and the cross-members are of similar material. Many readers have asked about the cooling system. An opening is left behind the driving seat, as will be seen from the side elevation, so that an air scoop can direct a current of air straight on to the cylinders. This is simple and certainly efficient, for the engine keeps just as cool as it would do if mounted in the frame of a motor cycle. Observe that the engine and gearbox are carried on engine plates, bolted between the two main members by means of long bolts with suitable distance tubes for location purposes. In order to brace the two rear members and keep them in alignment a long U bolt with angle pieces brazed at each corner are used, and the rocking members which carry the rear wheel are covered with a washer plate at the rear extremities; bushes are placed through to suit the rear-wheel spindles. A detail of this is shown. The petrol tank can conveniently consist of a standard petrol tin.

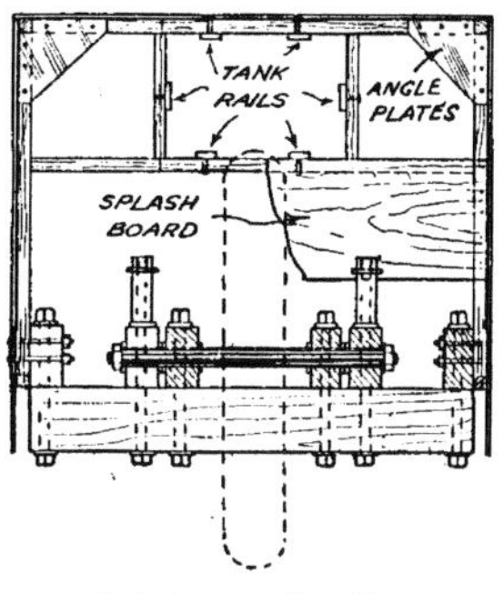

End view across line AB.

Lubrication

Lubrication is by means of the pump incorporated with the engine and which merely needs to be coupled up with a small oil tank with a tap soldered into the bottom. This is conveniently mounted through one of the bearers as shown. Mild steel angle brackets could be used to connect the various wooden members together.

I have shown the position of the steering and the wheels dotted, but it will be appreciated that the position of the front wheels is provisional only, and will depend upon the type of front axle which is employed. Scale drawings of the axle will be given next month, together with details of the body, seating, and finishing. The screen, as I mentioned last month, is the Auster type, and steering wheels can be purchased from Bluemels. I shall also include next month actual photographs of the completed car.

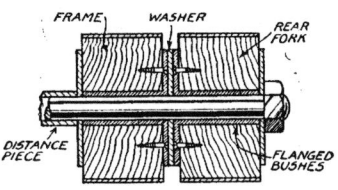

The rear frame members are bushed to take the rear fork pivot.

The whole of the wooden structure forming the chassis will be apparent from the side and plan views. In selecting the wood, insist upon straight-grained material free from knots and shakes. Ash must be used—no other wood is suitable to resist the stresses imposed by the engine. You will save yourself a lot of disappointment by adhering to the specification, and using ash. Most coach-builders will supply it or get it for you.

Wherever possible use bolts. Where wood screws are essential use a small drill to give a leading hole, and dip the point of the screws in vaseline before inserting them. This will prevent rust and make it easy for the screws to be removed. Ash is a hard wood, and any attempt to force a screw home will result in a mutilated head and a screw which cannot be removed. Where two parts are to be screwed together the top part should have a clearing hole so that the head of the screw can draw the two parts together.

Croid or Seccotine are admirable as glues. Where a large surface is to be covered the wood should first be warmed and the glue itself heated in hot water to render it more fluid. After the two parts are glued they should be placed under pressure for several hours until the glue has set. When using a bradawl make sure that you insert the blade with its cutting edge at right angles to the grain. This will avoid splitting. Use coach-maker's panel pins and oval section brads for nailing purposes. Such should be at least ¾ in. long, otherwise they will vibrate loose.

Where possible use Whitworth or B.S.F. bolts. Do not use stove or gutter bolts as the threads are not sufficiently accurately cut and the nuts will vibrate off. Locking washers should be used under the nuts securing the engine and gearbox plates. The bolts should be of the castellated type and split pins must be used to secure the nuts.

Metal straps should be of 16-gauge mild steel plate of the bright rolled variety. Tinned iron is unsuitable; for the spacing and distance tubes use bright drawn steel tube of 16 gauge; the ends, of course, must be cut square, and the tubes should be a reasonable fit on the bolts to prevent the latter from bending.

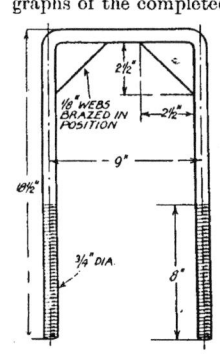

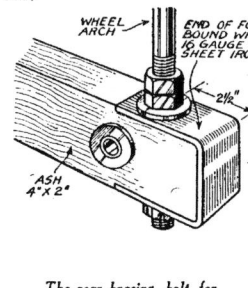

The rear bracing bolt for the rear "fork" member.

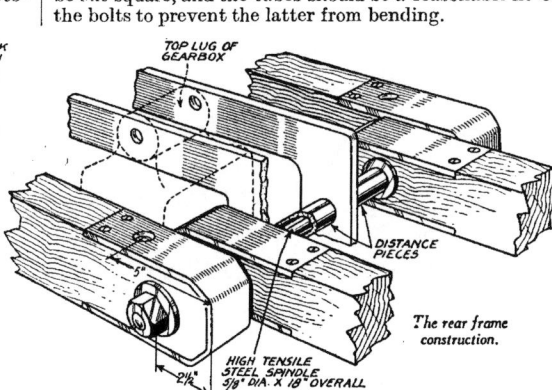

The rear frame construction.

Building our £20 Car

THE PRACTICAL MECHANICS £20 CAR

By F. J. Camm

ALL RIGHTS RESERVED

Final Constructional Details. Previous Articles on this Fascinating and Easily Built Three-Wheeler Appeared in our Issues dated March, April, and May. Blueprints are now Available. The Designer, Mr. F. J. Camm, grants a Free Licence to Every Reader to Build One

The finished £20 car.

I SHOW this month photographs and drawings which will enable the reader to complete this fascinating little vehicle, of which many hundreds are being built from details in this journal. Before dealing with them I should like to dispose of a further batch of queries. Firstly, regarding insurance. Several readers have asked whether there will be any difficulty about this. I have accordingly been in touch with several insurance companies, none of whom have any objection to insuring the car. Messrs. Premier Motor Policies tell me that they are prepared to issue a third-party insurance policy for £3 7s. 6d., and I recommend readers to get into touch with them.

Registration

An important point occurs regarding registration. In the item on Form RF1, which must be filled in in order to obtain the necessary registration numbers, there is a line reading "maker's name." I have been in touch with the London County Council on this point, and would inform readers they must enter the make as "Camm." The registration figures assigned to my own car are CXR547, and if any reader should spot me on the road do not hesitate to stop me if you wish to ask any questions and inspect my vehicle. I expect in the near future, as time permits, to embark upon a series of timed runs, of which I shall disclose details in due course.

Many readers are asking where they can get fittings made, and I have accordingly arranged with several manufacturers for this to be done at nominal prices. I can let you have these addresses upon application if you will enclose a stamped and addressed envelope. You will appreciate, of course, that the price of the finished car may come out a little higher than £20, if you elect to have some of the parts made, although £20 is actually on the high side.

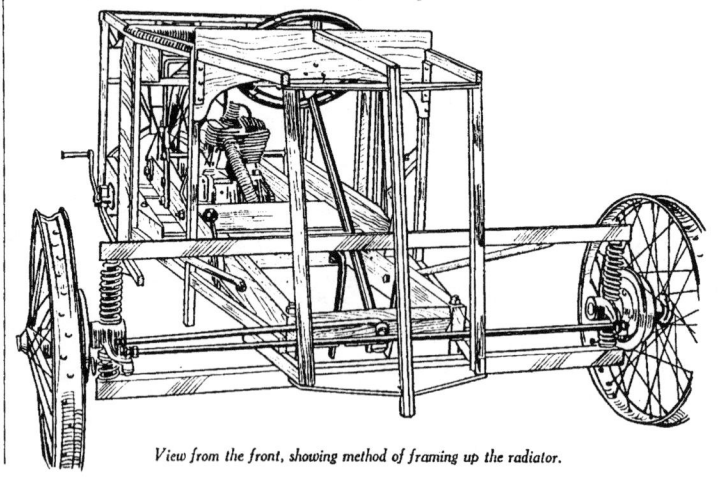

View from the front, showing method of framing up the radiator.

The £20 3-Wheeled Car of 1936

A FOUR-WHEELED MIDGET CAR

By F. J. CAMM

Modifications of the Design for our £20 Three-Wheeler Described in Recent Issues of this Journal.

A PERSPECTIVE SKETCH OF THE MIDGET CAR WITH PART OF THE BODYWORK CUT AWAY TO SHOW THE INTERNAL CONSTRUCTION.

LAST year I described in a series of articles the construction of a Midget Three-Wheeled Car powered by an air-cooled single cylinder motor-cycle engine of a capacity up to 500 c.c. Very many cars have been built from those designs, blue prints for which are still available at 10s. 6d. per set. They have all performed very satisfactorily on the road, and the constructors have written me enthusiastic letters paying tribute to the simplicity of the construction and the reliability of the little vehicle on the road. It was designed to give the performance of a motor-cycle but the weather protection of a car, and this object it fulfilled admirably. I have published photographs of some of the cars built from my drawings, and readers will be able to gauge from those as well as from the photographs of my own car the practicability of the design.

A Monocar

It was, however, a monocar, and many readers wrote asking whether they could widen the body to accommodate a passenger. I advised them against this, since the chassis members and other parts would have needed considerable modification to have made the car strong and roadworthy.

Ever since the conclusion of the series of articles I have received a steady flow of correspondence asking me to prepare a design on somewhat similar lines suitable as a two-seater. I have given a great amount of thought to the matter, and decided that such a design would not be satisfactory as a three-wheeler, and accordingly I set about preparing a design for a four-wheeler but adopting a somewhat similar form of construction as for the three-wheeler. Therefore, it will not be necessary for me to go over that ground again, and I would refer readers desirous of building the present design to those articles which appeared in our issues dated March to August, 1936, back numbers of which are still available.

The Engine

The present car will need a more powerful engine, and I suggest one of at least 500 c.c. but preferably 750 c.c. Either a single cylinder or a twin cylinder will do. A motor-cycle gearbox of the 3-speed type and suitable for the engine should also be obtained. The top gear ratio should be 7 : 1 to prevent the engine from overheating, and as with the three-wheeler, an air chute underneath the seats should direct a blast of air direct on to the cylinder.

Additionally, wheels fitted with at least 3 in. tyres should be used. Motor-cycle sidecar wheels with internal expanding brake hubs should be employed, and it will be a comparatively simple matter to couple the brake operating mechanism so that all wheels are braked simultaneously. The body is constructed as before from three-ply, but the framing allows of variation in body form to please individual pleas. In many ways this four-wheeler is simpler to build than the three-wheeler since it dispenses with the rocking bar type of rear suspension, and makes use of standard ½ elliptic springs. These may be picked up quite cheaply from car breakers and by a suitable modification of the eye end they can be made to accommodate the live axle. I have not deemed it necessary owing to the comparatively narrow wheel track to employ differential gear. It will be remembered that some of the light cars of a few years ago, notably the Bleriot Whippet, did not employ a differential, although the wheel track was much wider than in the present case.

It will be seen that I have arranged the seating accommodation further back, which has necessitated a corresponding increase in the wheelbase. The same system of direct steering is employed this has been found after long experiment quite satisfactory on the three-wheeler. It should be even more so on a four-wheeler. The front suspension is the same, and consists of coil springs with snubber springs underneath.

The £20 4-Wheeled Midget Car of 1936

F.J.'s other Practical Journals

In addition to the *Hobbies* and the renowned *Practical Wireless* (1932), *Practical Mechanics* (1933) and *Practical Motorist* (re-started 1954) was: *The Practical Householder*. This was established in 1955, one shilling and three pence monthly (6¼p). This post war projected was directed at D.I.Y. householders interested in house decoration and repair.

F.J. once stated that *Householder* was his greatest triumph, with a circulation in October 1958 "approaching a million – and twice exceeding it". There was a *Practical Householder* Exhibition from 11th February 1958 until 1st March "Entry two shillings and 6d (12½p) at Earls Court".

Practical Engineering was a companion journal to *Practical Mechanics* (4d weekly).

```
The National DO-IT-YOURSELF MAGAZINE—LARGEST CIRCULATION!
The
PRACTICAL HOUSEHOLDER
EDITED BY F. J. CAMM
November Issue Now On Sale    PRICE 1/3

Double Glazing; A Low Cost Loft Ladder; Repairing Burst
Pipes with Plastic; Laying Cork Flooring; Lock Repairing;
Installing a Ground Floor Toilet; A Modern Room Screen;
Fixing Tiled Hardboard; Give Your Sewing Machine a Modern
Look; Cutting Rafters; A Coal Delivery Hatch; Continuous
Burning Fires; Unique Design for a Chair; Fitting Your Own
Fireback Boiler; A Useful Ironing Board; Restoring Oil
Paintings; Preparing Your House for Winter; Frost Pre-
cautions; Heating an Airing Cupboard; A Combined Leg-rest,
Foot Stool and Fireside Stool; House Insulation; Making a
Simple Wardrobe; Wolf Home Power Equipment.
Also included are regular features: Your Queries Answered; The P.H. Test Reports;
Letters to the Editor; Fred Theed's Page; and Passing It On.
```

The Cyclist. This was an early casualty of the war, becoming a supplement to *Practical Mechanics*, where it remained – under F.J.'s nom de plume, "Wayfarer" – until his death.

Home Movies also had to be temporarily accommodated in *Practical Mechanics* – as was *Practical Motorist*, due to paper shortages. These were a headache for F.J. for years after the war ended. His nom de plume was usually "Wayfarer".

Practical Photographer returned as a 16 page pull-out supplement to *Practical Mechanic* in July 1958. Below is a typical advertisement for *Practical Mechanics* (November 1957) from *Practical Motorist*.

```
You will enjoy our companion
monthly magazine—
"PRACTICAL
MECHANICS"
October Issue Now On Sale
Price 1/3

Principal Contents:
A Bedside Table; An Electric Pottery
Kiln; A Baby Alarm; Setting and
Sharpening Saws; A Useful Toolshed;
Netting for Beginners; A Photographic
Safe-light and Printer; A Model Scenic
Railway; A Touch-operated Electric
Fence Control Circuit; A Catapult
Gun; and regular features including
The Junior Chemist, Science Notes,
Trade Notes, and The Cyclist.
```

Practical Television started in March 1950.

F.J. once wrote for *Amateur Wireless* until this merged with *Practical Wireless*. For a time his columns appeared under the title *Practical and Amateur Wireless*.

Some of F.J.'s publications are now less rare than others, those with editions running into double figures include:

Workshop Calculations, Tables and Formulae	(+10 editions)
Practical Wireless Encyclopaedia	(13 editions)
Practical Wireless Circuits	(+17 editions)
Practical Wireless Service Manual	(11 editions)
Radio Engineers' Pocket Book	(+12 editions)
Newnes Engineers' Reference Book	(+10 editions)
Every Man's Wireless Book	(+13 editions)

Some popular publications such as *Beginner's Guide to Radio* continued after F.J.'s death in 1959 under another editor, Gordon J. King. His *Television and Short Wave Handbook* (1939) was published by Fortuny in U.S.A. in *Radio Craft*, price $2.50 cents.

> TELEVISION AND SHORT-WAVE HANDBOOK, by F. J. Camm (1939). Published by Fortuny. Size 5½ x 8 ins., cloth cover, 130 illustrations, 272 pgs. Price $2.50.
> A well-known English writer presents in 2 sections a "lavishly illustrated volume" which deals both theoretically and practically with every branch of television. The second section of the book discusses the elements in shortwave technique having particular bearing on television transmission and reception. Radio men may want to use this book as a reference for its 61-pg. dictionary of television terms. This dictionary also should make clear to the radio student any terms used in the text. We recommend Camm's new book.

Newnes Short Wave Manual was retailed widely outside the U.K., as by Angus & Robertson, Castleragh Street, Sydney, Australia in 1940.

His *Watches, Adjustment and Repair* (Newnes, six shillings (30p), 1940) was reviewed in a full column in *John O'London's Weekly*. It was described as "... the last word in modern watch technique".

F.J.'s *Practical Handyman*, price £5.00 was published by Newnes in two volumes as a complete Handyman D.I.Y.

Newnes Home Mechanic series included in the 1920's *The Home Woodworker* also *Model Aeroplanes and Airships* and *25 Simple Working Models*. F.J. edited *The Handyman's Enquire Within* which developed into *Practical Handyman*.

Link House Publications had previously printed *Carpentry for Amateurs*, price 2/6 in their *Practical Books for the Handyman* series. F.J. Camm's family collection includes a copy, and it appears he was concerned in some way.

He had many facets. There was F.J. the meticulous draughtsman and religious knowledge prize winner at school; the model aeroplane builder and reporter who developed into a versatile model maker. A keen cyclist and a quick study, following the same values of thrift and hard work that his father instilled in all his children – in different days he would have been able to gain a place at a university, when undoubtedly he would have shown his diligence and maturity.

The strong "Practical" streak and workshop experience is obvious in his writings on mechanical engineering, as a fitter, turner, pattern maker, foundry man, millwright and technical student, not forgetting watchmaker and leather worker. Possibly the "arts" were neglected, and he does not seem to have relaxed with golf as did Sydney.

His book of Workshop Calculations became a "must" for servicemen during the last war, needing many editions. Much of his leisure was spent in research and model making. He specialised particularly in wireless and mechanical engineering, but cycling, motoring, photography, classical music – and later radar and television – were mastered.

Some of his articles that were published in the technical press he reused in books. For sheer quantity and quality his output as Editor for Newnes and previous publishers is outstanding. These journals are becoming difficult to obtain, although some bound volumes exist, and odd numbers are still cherished. It has been calculated that the seven major series of journals he edited comprise over 5,000 editions, and with his output of over 100 books he is credited with millions of words.

The number of editions of his books sometimes exceeded a dozen. His name became a household word – the demand for his books and journals mostly written in non-technical language brought him customers all over the world, with translations into other languages and even Braille – and some pirating in the U.S.A.

Practical Wireless is now published by a new publisher who celebrated its 60 years of publication in 1992 in a supplement "The man behind it all" by Joan Ham.

Practical Mechanics is equally well known, but the companion *Practical Engineering* less so. *Practical Householder*, *Practical Motorist* and *Practical Television* – a post war effort – sold in thousands of copies. The advertisements he included in these journals gave valuable publicity to F.J.'s books as they were published, and to his "blue print" service.

Wartime paper constrictions resulted in temporary amalgamations of titles. He seems to have overcome staff shortages with work under pseudonyms. He could be described as a workaholic and certainly he was to be found in his office when the rest of George Newnes was shut for the weekend.

F.J. was familiar with B.S.A. and 'New Imperial' motor cycles which he wrote about for Pitmans Motor Cycle Library, complete with meticulous drawings.

F.J. was the writer of several books on motoring and diesel engines, and became Editor of *Practical Motoring*, which flourished for several years under Newnes.

The need for *More Miles Per Gallon* – the title of his wartime (1939) publication stemmed from rationing which started on 23rd September 1939. He advised on practical economy measures – and possible alternative fuels such as producer gas from wood, or coal gas carried in bags. There were tales of distilling alcohol from grain, or even brandy being used to get a car home that had run out of petrol! These tales lost nothing in the telling. F.J.'s advice was printed in the *Austin* car magazine and received good reviews.

There was a demand for information about diesel engines, and F.J. produced *Modern Oil Engine Practice as Applied to Stationary, Marine or Traction Diesels* in which he co-operated with experts in their various fields.

His own *Diesel Vehicles* went into six or more editions between 1940 and 1957.

Practical Engineering

This was published as a companion journal to *Practical Mechanics,* but disappeared possibly due to a wartime paper economy. F.J. brought together the information and references required by engineering specialists in separate craft books, and these were amalgamated in *Newnes Engineers Reference Book* first published in 1946, edited by F.J. Camm.

This was a great success but had to be updated and new editions published almost annually, one reason being the stream of British Standards that were being produced, making old standards obsolete. F.J. tended to keep the old standards in the volumes, as some firms still used them.

Workshop mathematics had become commonly needed, as the science of mechanics developed, and his books were consulted on the shop floor. As a result the later editions increased in size and weight to over 3½ pounds ... with a valuable display of advertisements, and a meticulous index.

F.J.'s "P.M. Blueprint" Service

THE P.M. BLUEPRINT SERVICE	THE P.M. BLUE-PRINT SERVICE
12 FT. ALL-WOOD CANOE.* New Series. No. 1. 3s. 6d. 10-WATT MOTOR. New Series.* No. 2. 3s. 6d. COMPRESSED-AIR MODEL AERO ENGINE.* New Series. No. 3. 5s. AIR RESERVOIR FOR COMPRESSED-AIR AERO ENGINE. New Series. No. 3a. 1s. "SPORTS" PEDAL CAR.* New Series. No. 4. 5s. F. J. CAMM'S FLASH STEAM PLANT.* New Series. No. 5. 5s. SYNCHRONOUS ELECTRIC CLOCK. New Series. No. 6. 5s.* ELECTRIC DOOR-CHIME. No. 7. 3s. 6d.* ASTRONOMICAL TELESCOPE. New Series. No. 8 (2 sheets). 7s.* CANVAS CANOE. New Series. No. 9. 3s. 6d.* DIASCOPE. New Series. No. 10. 3s. 6d.* EPISCOPE. New Series. No. 11. 3s. 6d.* PANTOGRAPH. New Series. No. 12. 1s. 6d.* COMPRESSED-AIR PAINT SPRAYING PLANT New Series No. 13. 7s. 6d.* £20 CAR* (Designed by F. J. CAMM), 10s. 6d. per set of four sheets. MASTER BATTERY CLOCK* Blueprints (2 sheets), 3s. 6d. Art board dial for above clock, 1s. OUTBOARD SPEEDBOAT 10s. 6d. per set of three sheets. SUPER-DURATION BIPLANE* Full-size blueprint, 2s. The 1-c.c. TWO-STROKE PETROL ENGINE* Complete set, 7s. 6d. STREAMLINED WAKEFIELD MONOPLANE—3s. 6d. LIGHTWEIGHT MODEL MONOPLANE Full-size blueprint, 3s. 6d. P.M. TRAILER CARAVAN* Complete set, 10s. 6d. P.M. BATTERY SLAVE CLOCK*—2s. The above blueprints are obtainable, post free, from Messrs. George Newnes, Ltd., Tower House, Southampton Street, Strand, W.C.2. An denotes constructional details are available, free, with the blueprint.	12FT. ALL-WOOD CANOE. New Series. No. 1, 3s. 6d.* 10-WATT MOTOR. New Series. No. 2, 3s. 6d.* COMPRESSED-AIR MODEL AERO ENGINE. New Series. No. 3, 5s.* AIR RESERVOIR FOR COMPRESSED-AIR AERO ENGINE. New Series. No. 3a, 1s. "SPORTS" PEDAL CAR. New Series. No. 4, 5s.* F. J. CAMM'S FLASH STEAM PLANT. New Series. No. 5, 5s.* SYNCHRONOUS ELECTRIC CLOCK. New Series. No. 6, 5s.* ELECTRIC DOOR-CHIME. No. 7, 3s. 6d.* ASTRONOMICAL TELESCOPE. New Series. Refractor. Object glass 3in. diam. Magnification x 80. No. 8 (2 sheets), 7s.* CANVAS CANOE. New Series. No. 9, 3s. 6d.* DIASCOPE. New Series. No. 10, 3s. 6d.* EPISCOPE. New Series. No. 11, 3s. 6d.* PANTOGRAPH. New Series. No. 12, 1s. 6d.* COMPRESSED-AIR PAINT SPRAYING PLANT. New Series. No. 13, 7s. 6d.* MASTER BATTERY CLOCK.* Blue-prints (2 sheets), 3s. 6d. Art board dial for above clock, 1s. OUTBOARD SPEEDBOAT. 10s. 6d. per set of three sheets. LIGHTWEIGHT MODEL MONOPLANE. Full-size blue-print, 3s. 6d. P.M. TRAILER CARAVAN. Complete set, 10s. 6d.* P.M. BATTERY SLAVE CLOCK, 2s. "PRACTICAL TELEVISION" RECEIVER (3 sheets), 10s. 6d. P.M. CABIN HIGHWING MONOPLANE. 1s.* P.M. TAPE RECORDER* (2 sheets), 5s. The above blue-prints are obtainable, post free, from Messrs. George Newnes, Ltd., Tower House, Southampton Street, Strand, W.C.2. An * denotes constructional details are available free with the blue-prints.

Practical Mechanics Blueprint Service

The above was a popular service that F.J. provided for a stamped addressed envelope and three penny stamps, also a "query" coupon.

Apart from electrical queries – which service was discontinued in 1950 without explanation – almost any query received a detailed reply in the columns of Newnes *Practical Mechanics*. The advice was not infallible – in January 1950 he advised someone wishing to insulate the interior of corrugated iron huts (Nissen huts) to use asbestos fibre to be obtained from Turner Brothers Asbestos Co. Ltd., of Rochdale. Alternatively he suggested a "new material, a sort of spun glass, which has been named 'Fibreglass'".

While F.J. provided free blue-prints with *Practical Wireless*, a series of *Practical Mechanics* blueprints were available for small sums.

Practical Motorist

The present series dates from 1955, (there were earlier editions killed by paper shortages in wartime) and was another of the *Practical* series to cost one shilling and five pence (6¼ pence). In May 1994 the present publishers could claim "60 years of Practical Motoring", with acknowledgements of F.J.'s first 27 years as editor. There had been several competitors, *The Autocar, The Motor* – dating from 1909. At one time the titled include "& Motor Cyclist". *Practical Motorist* would have a stand at the Motor Show at Earls Court – which F.J. said he attended "incognito" – a practice he followed sometimes at other shows.

Like the earlier Amalgamated Press competitor, it included information about useful – and sometimes otherwise – accessories and fitments, servicing advice for popular makes and data sheets for "Cars for which Handbooks are unobtainable" including pre-war cars, many of which were still on the road in 1957.

There had been fuel restrictions, and petrol economy was a feature. "Readers' queries" was a popular feature, the "free advice" of earlier journals, for which a coupon from the appropriate journal was required. The latter was under the heading "Conducted by Ivor Clew", which needs forgiveness.

Car breakers' spares and services were in the "classified" advertisements with remould and retread tyres. The journal tells much about the pros and cons of car ownership and D.I.Y. needs of those days.

As was his practice, F.J. used space to advertise the other *Practical* journals, *Practical Mechanics*, *Practical Householder* – which claimed "the largest circulation" and the new *Practical Home Money Maker*.

F.J.'s *Practical Motorist's Encyclopaedia* was first published by Newnes in 1935, with later editions up to the ninth in 1958, just before he died.

The 1919 Cambro car, and the 1936 "Three wheeler for £20" also the 1937 four-wheeled midget car (described earlier above) were never mentioned in *Practical Motorist* but F.J. referred to "Our £20 Car" in his *Practical Mechanics* "Silver Jubilee" review in October 1958.

He queried Scotland Yard for explanations and recommendations and reported these in *On the Road* by Waysider or Wayfarer. Similarly the A.A. were helpful e.g. concerning the new Radar Speedmeter (November 1957).

Practical Home Money Maker

First published in October 1957, *Practical Home Money Maker* may be regarded as F.J.'s swansong. As can be seen from the advertisement for No 2, he seems to have resurrected some of the articles – and profitable hobbies – of previous years.

Practical Home Money Maker

The Practical Series

The *Practical* series that F.J. edited included:

Practical Wireless (1932)   *Practical Mechanics (1933)*
Practical Motorist and Motor Cyclist (1934)   *Practical Television (1950)*
Practical Householder (1956)   *Practical Home Money Maker* (1957)

All were published monthly (in 1958) price one shilling and three pence each ($^1/_{16}$th £1), *Practical Photographer* was in July 1958 a supplement to *Practical Mechanics* which celebrated its 25th birthday.

F.J. goes to Law

He was always prepared to defend his work – as in May 1930, when the editor of the Society of Model Aeronautical Engineers Society, Mr W.E. Evans, published an "Open Letter" addressed to F.J. Camm. This was critical and somewhat rude concerning a letter F.J. had addressed to the correspondence columns of *Flight* disparaging the S.M.A.E. formula about fuselage proportions for models. The formula apparently had the purpose of eliminating the "flying stick" favoured by F.J. who threatened to take action against Mr Evans. The latter published in the next issue "desire to unreservedly withdraw my imputation which I may unwittingly have made against Mr F.J. Camm and to offer his my sincere apologies for the annoyance I have caused him". This apology went on to explain that the letter F.J. complained about was written on Mr Evans' own responsibility and in no way represented the views of the S.M.A.E.

This matter had caused F.J. considerable indignation, as he had been one of the founder members of the Model Aeronautical Engineers Society shortly after the end of the 1914-18 war, when F.J. edited the model section of *Flight* and had collected the cups and trophies of the defunct Kite and Model Aeroplane Association as well as securing that the L.A.M.A. (London Aero Models Association) changed its name to the S.M.A.E. responsible for rules governing the sport. With the other founder members F.J. is remembered by model flyers who benefit from their foresight.

Not all his contemporary writers were in agreement with F.J.'s views – towards the later years of his life some regarded his works, especially on model aircraft, as dated or even extremely antiquated, and not reflecting progress. Perhaps he tended to live in the past, but after his death, his publications were revised and reissued under the names of other editors (e.g. Fenton's *Diesel Vehicles*, and Naylor's *Newnes Engineers' Pocket Book of Tables 1964*, also *Practical Wireless Service Manual, 1960*, as Periodical Publications. His *Radio Engineers' Pocket Book* was later published under Collins, Albert T. This would have been F.J.'s 13th edition. But there is no doubt that F.J. was an important figure in British modelling and technical publishing history, and his work deserves to be looked at in detail.

Legal Notes

It is significant that *Practical Motorist and Motor Cyclist* (November 1957) included half a page of legal notes "By a Barrister" with a warning in F.J.'s leading article about "The New Magistrates' Court Act". I have not found any instance of F.J. losing a case, or legal argument. This may mean that he was always in the right – or had access to superior legal advice.

A writ from a magicians' Union was received after he exposed a number of tricks – but F.J.'s advice (or was it George Newnes?) on legal matters was such that the writs were withdrawn – there is no copyright in a trick as such.

In 1944 he forced the Bernards Publishers Ltd. to withdraw their *Manual of Metals and Alloys* and their *Radio Manual*, as infringements of his own works *Dictionary of Metals and Alloys* also his *Newnes*

Engineers' Pocket Book, *Practical Wireless Service Manual* and *Radio Engineers' Vest Pocket Book* with a substantial sum for damages. He suffered pirating in the U.S.A. but does not appear to have been able to proceed.

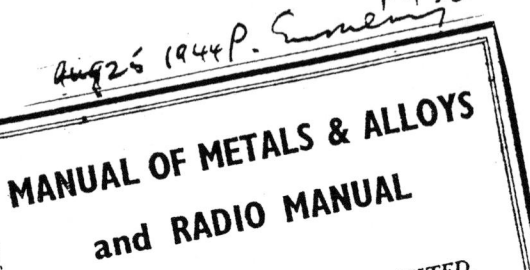

Infringements resulting in advertisements of regret, damages and costs

**Lord Brabazon (standing) with F.J. Camm to his left,
addressing the Bassett-Lowke 50th Anniversary Dinner in 1949**

The "Episode" is linked to the Bassett-Lowke 50th Anniversary Dinner (November 1949), when F.J. was a guest at the top table, where he sat next to the great Lord Brabazon of Tara, (numbered 1 above), whose entry in Who's Who is one of the longest – (termed the First English Aviator, he held No. 1 certificate granted by the Royal Aero Club for pilots, won the Daily Mail £1,000 for flying a circular mile on an all-English made aeroplane in 1909, Minister of Transport 1940-41 etc.)

The accounts of the dinner includes F.J. as "Editor, *Practical Mechanics*" and that the toasts included "Gentlemen of the Press" by R.H. Fuller. (Roland Fuller wrote the *Bassett-Lowke Story*, which he dedicated to Henry Greenly "who did so much for Bassett-Lowke and scale model railways".)

In front of F.J. is a scale model of the Bassett-Lowke "Flying Scotsman", possibly the one he built from a Bassett-Lowke kit, and wrote a pamphlet of directions.

"F.J. responded for the Press" (*Newnes Practical Mechanics*, January 1950) and included an account of the dinner in his notes, but did not mention the matter in *Practical Wireless*.

F.J. sometimes worked with Henry Greenly in connection with the latter's *Model, Railways and Locomotives* – a novel and imaginative monthly magazine with items of scientific and general interest culled from world-wide sources, to quote from *The Miniature World of Henry Greenly*. This discussed the Channel Tunnel proposal and jet engines for aeroplanes, years before these took shape. F.J. sometimes contributed articles regarding model aeroplanes. When Greenly's magazine merged with *Everyday Science* F.J. contributed. His own *Marvels of Modern Science* was published in 1935 and a revised edition in 1938. At this time he was editing a number of magazines for Newnes and his books included several on model aeroplanes.

The Greenly Episode

About 1938 Greenly appears to have been irritated by what he thought was "pirating of my designs" by F.J. To give vent to his feelings, Greenly wrote to Bassett-Lowke alleging that F.J. was using his drawings without permission, and then let the matter rest. Bassett-Lowke may have thought he was implicated with one of the alleged pirated designs and showed the letter to F.J. who stalked off with the letter – which he refused to give up – in deep umbrage, saying he was bringing an action for libel. Both sides prepared their cases, and were confident of success, but Greenly's solicitors advised him to withdraw, as his chance of proving his case was less than 50%, and he might have been held liable not only for his own costs but also those of F.J.

In the event, Greenly lost, the case being undefended, and F.J. obtained £500 damages. As Greenly was in financial difficult at the time, he went bankrupt as a result. However, Greenly did not bear a grudge. He met F.J. and buried the hatchet, shaking hands. Of course, the lawyers were the principal winners.

At this time, F.J.'s wife was ill – she died in 1939 – and war conditions and paper shortages were causing difficulties for F.J.'s magazines and books.

F.J. Relaxes

He was a generous "uncle" to the younger Camms and nieces and nephews – the latter received copies of *Hobbies* Annuals at Christmas and birthdays. He designed his own Christmas cards, a set of these are in the Windsor Collection. One shows "F.J. The Practical This" and the "Practical That" and the "Practical Anything Man". Another – the penultimate – shows himself as Father Christmas showering around money from a sack marked "Practical Home Money Maker". It is signed "Love from Fred and Freddie". His only son Freddie might have felt to be in the shadow of his famous uncle Sydney, and popular editor father.

F.J. and Freddie's Christmas card, 1957

Few family groups have been found. One shows F.J. with his wife Dorothy May and "Little Fred" with bucket and spade, sitting on the sand accompanied by a girl. All are warmly dressed, and it is hardly a Summer "Happy Snap".

F.J. Camm and Mrs Dorothy May (Field) Camm and Little Fred (Frederick William Sydney Camm) in bucket and spade days (with Mrs Camm's sister?)

The Ostrich Inn, Colnbrook

In later years, F.J. would relax at the Colnbrook inn, "The Ostrich". A self taught musical virtuoso, he would play the banjo – or a pianoforte duet with his old friends and BBC 2L0 pianist Cecil Panting, whose small son Bob recalls F.J.'s Jaguar car, of which he was very proud – and the chiming watch which F.J. repaired. He was regarded as the "best repairer of chiming pocket watches". One he fitted into a gold case, marked "F.J.C.", which is being sought. His book on watch and clock repairs published in 1940 by George Newnes was well received in the horological world.

This work appears to stem from the capabilities of his workshop, with its lathe and equipment with which F.J. could prepare rough castings and other parts from Bassett-Lowke and Stuart Turner of Henley for his mechanical models. No doubt this work gave F.J. great pleasure, but there was not always profit to be made – he sometimes said that he had "champagne tastes with a sherbert income".

"The Ostrich" had historical interest for F.J., especially the ancient tales of the murders that the landlord once arranged with a bed which he could tip up so that the wealthy traveller could be dropped into a boiling cauldron, robbed, and the body put in the Colne river. The model that F.J. made – with a mattress made by Cecil Panting – was kept on view in the bar, after being inaugurated by the Marquis of

Donegal in 1950, F.J.'s wireless article friend – F.J. was his Best Man at the Marquis's wedding. F.J. published a book about the Ostrich and its infamous bed.

His model was reviewed by the *Windsor Express* (1st December 1950).

The Ostrich Inn, Colnbrook, Murder Bed

His niece Dorothy Dickson writes

"F.J. was a jolly, good natured uncle, very interested in classical music. He was a keen amateur pianist".

F.J. could be a convivial man – he acquired his own "quaich" – a two handled drinking cup. This could be filled with malt whisky, and some say should be drained then turned upside down to prove it had been properly emptied. His quaich is dated 1913 and is of sterling silver.

He was an excellent after dinner speaker, a member of the Royal Society of Arts, and White's club. He was asked to speak on behalf of journalists, as at the Bassett-Lowke 50th Anniversary dinner.

The Camms and the V.E. Day Celebrations, May 1945

Prime Minister Winston Churchill declared in a broadcast message that 8th May 1945 was to be a National Holiday, and the whole country went on the spree.

There were a series of bonfires, celebrations for the children, impromptu races in public parks, dancing in the streets to local bands and to pianos dragged out of houses. Despite shortages, there were "treats" for children who had long been deprived. Street parties were organised, and the Camms of Alma Road, Windsor had a huge party outside their house, as can be seen in the photograph dated 25th May in the *Windsor Express*. Germany had surrendered at last.

**V.E. 1945 Day, Saturday 19th May 1945
Many Camms present, including F.J.'s mother, brother, niece**

Everyone knew that Mr Sydney Camm was responsible for the design of the wonderful "Hurricane" fighter, which was said to be eight times more plentiful and effective than the "Spitfire", especially as hundreds of Hurricanes had been available due to action by Mr T.O.M. Sopwith and Mr Sydney Camm before the Spitfire was available in quantity. Hurricane pilots were proud of their staunchness after damage. The tables were arranged in a "V" formation outside number 10 Alma Road.

Mrs Marie Camm – the mother of Sydney and F.J. and ten other children – was invited to cut the three big iced cakes. There were the first iced cakes that many of the 90 or so children had ever seen, due to rationing. When it was realised that it would be Mrs Camm's birthday the following day, they all sang "Happy Birthday to you" and gave three cheers for Sydney and other members of the Camm family who were present, also for Mrs Clayton and Mr J.D. Brooks – an A.R.P. warden – who had arranged the party.

Everyone was especially proud of Mr Sydney Camm "who belonged to Windsor". A telegram was sent to the King and Queen which said "Your Majesties, the children of Alma Road and Arthur Road, Windsor and their parents send loyal and loving greetings from their V.E. party being held today. We sincerely hope that the war in the Far East will soon be ended so that a real peace will come to our beloved country. Long may you reign".

The King's Private Secretary replied "The King and Queen sincerely thank the children of Alma Road and Arthur Road, Windsor and their parents for their loyal greetings and good wishes from the Victory party".

Telegrams were read from relations serving elsewhere, the local Italian family Vettises somehow managed to resume making ice cream, and "Kay" a local conjuror and entertainer, gave a free show, which was voted a "clever exhibition". The children ran races and were given prizes of money. Mrs Matthews won the Mothers Race and Mr Abbott, manager of the adjacent Royal Windsor Gas light Co. lit the street that the children only knew as blacked out for the war. They could stay up late while their parents danced and sang popular songs. The funds left over were to be used to take the children to the sea side, that most of them had never seen because of war time restrictions.

But it was to be many anxious weeks before the dropping of atomic bombs on Japan brought V.J. Day, and the end of the long war, and their fathers and other men folk came home. Meanwhile there would be no more bombs, V1s or V2s, or siren air raid warnings.

F.J. The Model Maker

He was a fine model maker from the time he left school, when he (and Sydney) made many model aeroplanes good enough to sell to an Eton store, and, secretly, to Eton College boys. Later he made at least six superb models. After F.J. died intestate in February 1959, his eldest brother (now Sir Sydney Camm) distributed these models to male members of the family. George Camm seems to have acquired three, including a prize winning one-eighth scale model of the WERNER 218.5 c.c. motor cycle that F.J. saw on exhibition at the Science Museum, South Kensington in 1953/4. He used measured details to make the model that won the first prize in the Pioneer Class of the Autocycle Union 1954 Model Motor Cycle competition. The original Werner Motor cycle had a De Dion single cylinder four stroke air cooled engine which was attached to the cycle steering head and partially supported by reinforced front forks. A surface type carburettor with a wick vaporiser formed part of the small petrol tank. Ignition was by coil and accumulator.

The drive consisted of twisted strip rawhide round belt driving the front wheel via an inner rim attached to the 36 spokes. The weight was 65 pounds. Both wheels were 26 inch "of the Westwood type". The machine sold for £45. F.J. wrote a small illustrated pamphlet *The Story of the Werner* (16 pages, 4" x 3", publisher F.J. Camm, Tower House, Strand, WC22). This included a brief history of the Werner.

This model was sold by auctioneers (Phillips) after George Camm's death in 1987, and has not been traced.

F.J. also made a model of the first practical self propelled passenger vehicle using an internal combustion engine which was built by Carl Benz on 3rd July 1886. This was steered by a single wheel, and had a horizontal engine between the rear wheels, which were driven by belts. These could be shifted from a low speed pulley to a high speed, to act as a clutch and to "change gear". The final drive was by side chains and embodied an early differential. (A refinement that F.J. omitted from his "£20 car"). This model was also sold at auction, after George Camm's death.

A third model – a $2^{1}/_{2}$" gauge $^{1}/_{2}$" scale 4.6.2 LNER "Flying Scotsman" was made by F.J. using castings and parts from Bassett-Lowkes. This was given a place of honour at the Bassett-Lowkes 50th Anniversary dinner at the Savoy Hotel in front of the guest of honour, Lord Brabazon of Tara, on whose left sat F.J. Camm. He represented *Practical Mechanics* and gave the response to the toast "The Gentlemen of the Press". This model has not been traced. A fourth model was purchased by old boys (including George Camm) of F.J.'s old school (now Princess Margaret Royal Free School, Windsor) for £500 in

1989, where it is now kept, and was last exhibited at the F.J. Centenary Exhibition, Windsor from 17th November until 15th January 1996. It was made by F.J. from castings, patterns, drawings and partly finished parts and mechanism obtained from Bassett-Lowkes. This finished working model of a Burrell road tractor had been chromium plated after finishing on a lathe, with silver soldered water tube boiler, wheels, axles and flywheel checked for truth complete with brake drums and chimney. The scale is three quarters of an inch to the foot.

The section of a four cylinder engine built by F.J. Camm, even the spark plugs 'spark' when the handle is turned

His delightful miniature section of a four cylinder engine – in which even the sparking plugs "spark" when the starting handle is turned – is known to have been passed between other Camm neighbours until it reached someone who appreciates the careful workmanship but refuses to allow it to be exhibited. It has been traced to a Langley block of flats. This was one of F.J.'s best examples of workmanship.

The Burrell type traction engine, introduced by Bassett-Lowke Ltd. F.J. Camm's three-quarter inch scale model was purchased in 1989 by the Princess Margaret Royal Free School, Windsor by the Old Boys Association, led by George Camm

Practical Wireless celebrates 60 years of publication, October 1992

Under the heading "The Man behind F. J. Camm", Mrs Joan Ham, a freelance journalist, prepared in 1992, a six page supplement for *Practical Wireless*. Her exhaustive research has been a great help to me regarding F.J.'s wireless history, besides indicating where other research might be rewarding. I am most grateful to Mrs Ham for her help and advice. Copies of the celebratory issue can be obtained from: PW Publishing, Practical Wireless, Arrowsmith Court, Station Approach, Broadstone, Dorset. BH18 8PW.

Mrs Ham's husband donated his radio collection to the Amberley Museum, Chalkpits, near Arundel, BN18 9LT, which is well worth a visit. The museum has many of F.J.'s books and a full run of *Practical Wireless* from issue number 1, but the library is not usually available to the general public. Membership of the Museum is most useful, because of the many crafts and processes on display, with rides on the railway and vintage vehicles which children always enjoy, as well as the radio display.

F.J. The Editor – A Summary

1913-1915	Model Editor of *Flight*
1918-1922	Technical Editor of *Everyday Science*
	This began as Cassell & Co's *Amateur Wireless*
1919	Editor, Benn Brothers, *Aeronautics*
? 1920	Editor, *Aircraft & Flying* (vide *Aeromodeller*)
	= Model Flying Machines, 1918
? 1925	*Hobbies* Journals and Annuals
1932-1959	*Practical Wireless*
	(F.J. editor of combined *Amateur Wireless* & *Practical Wireless*, 26th January 1935)
	Reverts to *Practical Wireless* 1939 with new cover
1933-1959	*Practical Mechanics* (No. 1, October 1933)
1950	*Practical Television* (No. 1, 24th March 1950)
1936	(There had been a previous short-lived supplement *Practical Television* included in the title of *Practical Wireless* from 1936, discontinued September 1939)
Pre 1953	*The Cyclist*, *Practical Engineering*
	(Companion to *Practical Mechanics*)
1956	*Practical Householder*
1957	*Practical Home Money Maker* (No. 1, October 1957)
1934/5	*Practical Motorist*
	(60 years publication claimed in May 1994 edition)
	* *The Cyclist* became a supplement to *Practical Mechanics*, due to paper shortage. *Home Movies*, associated with *Practical Photography*, became another supplement in *Practical Mechanics* due to paper shortages.
	Practical Photography became a 16 page pull-out to *Practical Mechanics* in July 1958.
March 1959	F.J. Camm's name disappeared from the front covers of the *Practical* series for the first time since 1930s.

Periodicals associated with F.J. Camm

F.J.'s contribution to contemporary journals was prodigious, as is shown by the following list:

Flight	(pre 1915)
Models, Railways and Locomotives	(pre 1919)
Everyday Science	(1919-1924)
The Boys Own Paper	
George Newnes *Practical* Series	(1933-1959)

    Wireless, Mechanical Engineering, Household, Motorist, Television, Home Money Maker

Hobbies Journal and Annuals
Modern Boy
The Cyclist
Austin Magazine
Watchmaker and Jeweller

References

Reference has been made to the following:
"The Man Behind It All, F.J. Camm" (Mrs Joan Ham) PW Publishing Ltd. (1992)
The Miniature World of Henry Greenly (E.A. Steel and E.H. Steel, 1973)
Windsor Express
Windlesora Journals of the Windsor Local History Publications Group
Aero Manual 1909 (The Motor)
Patrick Y. Alexander biography (*Gordon Cullingham*) Cross Manufacturing Co (1938) Bath BA2 5RR
Aeromodeller
Books edited or written by F.J. Camm (See Appendix)

Libraries and Museums

Royal Aeronautical Society
The R.A.F. Museum, Colindale
Croydon, Slough, Windsor, Northampton Public libraries
The Science Museum
The British Museum
British Newspaper Museum, Colindale
United States Air Force Museum, Dayton, Ohio
Amberley Museum, West Sussex

Institutions with F.J. material in Library

The Institute of Civil Engineers
The Institution of Mechanical Engineers
The Institution of Electrical Engineers

F.J.'s editorships included:

Model Editor, *Flight*

Technical Editor, *Everyday Science, Hobbies, Practical Wireless, Practical Mechanics, Practical Engineering, The Cyclist, Practical Motoring, Practical Householder, Practical Moneymaker, Aeronautics, Aircraft and Flying*.

He also organised the model section of the Royal Aero Show until its cessation.

Following in F.J.'s Footsteps and the Obituaries

When he lived in Windsor and worked in London, F.J. would leave his house in Grove Road and hurry to the Windsor & Eton Riverside station for the train to Waterloo.

His friend and co-member of the Windsor Model Aero Club, Bob Mainwood would sometimes see him running for the train, clutching a case with his papers and lunch.

From Waterloo F.J. had several alternative routes to George Newnes offices in Southampton Street at Tower House. This prestigious building has seven floors, with F.J.'s editorial offices on the fifth floor.

George Newnes were taken over by Heinemann, and Butterworth, but it is not known what happened to F.J.'s reference library and books at Tower House. *Practical Wireless* and *Practical Motoring* survive at Broadstone, Dorset.

Practical Householder was bought by IPC Magazines in the sixties, then went to Maxwell Communications in the seventies and on to Headway Home and Law in the eighties. That company was taken over by Nexus Media Ltd. in 1994 and with it went the ownership of Practical Householder, which is now in its 40th year.

The direct route on foot from Waterloo to Tower House is via Hungerford Bridge – the pedestrian way alongside the railway into Charing Cross Station. After crossing the busy Strand, and turning eastwards, Southampton Street is soon reached. This runs from the Strand to Covent Garden. The Strand can of course be reached from Waterloo Bridge, or from the tube to the Embankment station.

On leaving Tower House and turning towards the Strand, one notices "The Coal Hole" immediately opposite – a convenient watering place. A few yards towards Charing Cross is Durham House Street with the Royal Society of Arts premises. F.J. was a member since his election in 1936 (when he gave his address as 27 Strathearn Avenue, Whitton, Twickenham) until 1948.

Strathearn Avenue is a short distance from Whitton Station. After his wife Dorothy May died in May 1939, and his only son Freddie in December 1957, it is only a short melancholy walk to Percy Road and the Hospital Bridge Road crossroads with its entrance to Twickenham Cemetery, where all three are in Section "M" plot 290.

F.J. was only 63 when he died. He employed a man servant and his wife at Whitton. It was rumoured that he would marry his secretary, but this was not to be.

After his wife diedin May 1939 and especially after his son "Little Fred" died, in 1957, F.J. seemed to have been mostly in his office at Tower House, Southampton Street, Strand in Newnes Technical Department. This was better known to the staff as Mr Camm's department. Here he was to be found on most Saturdays and some Sundays.

He died suddenly at home on Wednesday 18th February 1959, age 63, from bronchial pneumonia, after being taken ill in his office. He had been a heavy smoker.

The April 1959 issues of the *Practical* series missed his name from the front cover for the first time since the 1930's, and printed obituaries.

One of the last items that had taken his editorial attention was about safety belts. Early in 1959 the British Safety Council had issued their findings on over five months research into the practicability –

and feasibility – of fitting safety belts in cars. It was estimated that the compulsory fitting of such belts would save at least 700 lives a year, and reduce the severity of injuries to the driver and passengers. It was to be many years before safety belts became required by law.

Aeromodeller printed this obituary in their April 1959 edition:-

Passing of a Pioneer

"Frederick James Camm, editor of the George Newnes Practical *series of publications died on 18th February age 63 years. The aeromodelling movement will always owe a great deal to "F.J.C.", brother of Hawker's more famous Sir Sydney Camm, and indeed only last month in our Jubilee reminiscences it was recalled that the S.M.A.E. title was adopted on a proposition of his.*

His many sided interests as an horologist, cyclist, model engineer, radio technician and editor have tended to push into the background his aeromodelling activities.

When still in his teens before the 1914-18 war, he designed and built a petrol engine of considerable merit and later in 1932 produced one the earliest then subminiatures of 1.155 c.c. Another of his claims to aeromodelling fame was the introduction to this country in 1931 of the now ubiquitous balsawood.

Throughout his life he maintained a close and active interest in aeromodelling, holding at various times the model Editorship of Flight, Aeronautical Aircraft *and* Flying, *and organising the model section of the annual Royal Show until its cessation.*

As Editor of Practical Mechanics *he published regular articles on all aspects of modelling and only in recent months produced a most valuable publication on radio control. We knew him personally for 30 years and valued his praise and kindly criticism. We mourn his passing and will feel his loss."*

His funeral was at Twickenham Cemetery on 24th February 1959. The family grave is in Section M, first row, number 290. F.J. died intestate, and administration was granted to the National Provincial Bank. His brother Sir Sydney distributed F.J.'s models – one to each male Camm – and gave a special bookcase containing a library edition of leather bound volumes of some of his books to his sister in law, Mrs Kitty Camm at Woodley near Reading.

George Camm became the family archivist, and his house in Windsor was stacked with mementoes of Sir Sydney's successes, also F.J.'s journals, books and encyclopaedias. George's wife Ella had died, and the collection tended to become chaotic. He died suddenly in March 1987 and the archives seem to have been disposed of by the executors without any opportunity for salvage, except for a selection of Sydney's ephemera that George had allowed Berkshire Archives to acquire earlier.

Most of the models were subsequently sold at auction, and fetched high prices. The Royal Windsor Collection has recently acquired some books and "Camm" ephemera funded by the Royal Borough of Windsor & Maidenhead, plus some copies donated to the F.J. Camm Collection. Some of the Chartered Institution technical libraries have a few examples of F.J.'s books and the British Library has a list of over 100 which fill several pages of the catalogue. His books and journals are still collected by "F.J." fans. Generally the public libraries have relatively few examples of his work, but some booksellers have examples for sale.

His journals are rarely on offer, but his Wireless and Mechanics journals are to be found bound, sometimes in an amateurish manner.

There are examples of F.J.'s books and journals in the State library at Sydney N.S.W. Australia, and in Chicago.

There is a commemorative bronze plaque on the site of the W.M.A.C. shed at Ward Royal, Alma Road, Windsor – not easy to find – and this recalls Sydney's prowess. It is in the north-west corner, near to the junction of Alma Road and Arthur Road. A stone's throw away is 10 Alma Road which bears a

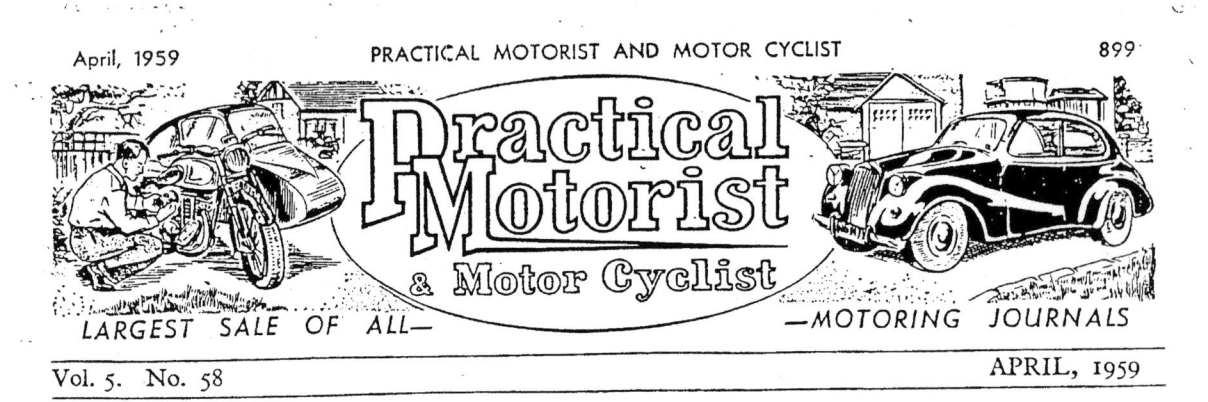

April, 1959   PRACTICAL MOTORIST AND MOTOR CYCLIST   899

Practical Motorist & Motor Cyclist

LARGEST SALE OF ALL— —MOTORING JOURNALS

Vol. 5. No. 58   APRIL, 1959

SAFETY BELTS

THE British Safety Council has recently issued the findings of a five-months research into the feasibility and practicability of safety belts in cars. Information and material was obtained from a number of countries which have produced and recommended safety belts, including the United States and Sweden. The Council claims that the compulsory fitting of such safety belts in cars would result in the saving of 700 lives a year and a 50 per cent reduction in the severity of injuries to drivers and passengers. It is estimated that 1,470 lives are lost annually as a result of car accidents in Britain, in addition to more than 100,000 injuries.

Research into the effectiveness of safety belts is also being carried out by the Road Research Laboratory, with the assistance of the police and the Medical Research Council; the Society of Motor Manufacturers and Traders is also considering safety features in motor vehicle design, including safety belts, and the British Standards Institution is setting up a committee to investigate the usefulness of a British standard for such apparatus.

With the advent of new motor-ways along which drivers will be able to maintain speeds of 60 to 80 miles an hour, this, we think, is a vital matter, and one which should be brought to the public eye. It has been established that when drivers and passengers are thrown around the interior of a vehicle involved in a collision, if the human body is held to the deceleration of the vehicle, as opposed to continuing in motion when the vehicle has actually stopped, the likelihood of certain types of injuries and fatalities is definitely reduced. It would also be safer than being thrown out through doors opened under the impact of a collision.

> It is with deepest regret that, as this issue goes to press, we have to inform readers of the sudden death of our Editor, Mr. F. J. Camm.
>
> For many years, Mr. Camm's name has been synonymous with the "Practical" Group of Journals, of which he was the originator, and the growth of which was largely due to his energetic and enthusiastic editorship.
>
> He was one of the first to realise that there was a public demand for practical journals written in non-technical language, and he met this demand by producing the Practical Group of magazines that made his name a household word. Mr. Camm's extensive knowledge as a scientist and engineer enabled him to write many technical books in the engineering and radio field.

Practical Motorist Obituary

slate plaque commemorating the "Hurricane" aeroplane Sydney designed. This plaque marks the house where F.J. and all 12 Camm children were born.

F.J. has no commemorative plaque, although the Royal Borough has the proposal for one under consideration. Meanwhile the Windsor Local History Publications Group with the Royal Borough of Windsor and Maidenhead are trying to collect examples of F.J.'s books and journals for the Royal Windsor Collection.

At the time of his death, he was concerned about increasing printing disputes developing. Normal publication of *Practical Mechanics* was prevented in June 1959, and publishing resumed in September 1959.

F.J. became a journalist while still at school, and emulated his elder brother Sydney in drafting reports about the Windsor Model Aeroplane Club to *Flight* in 1913-1915.

He must have been influenced – as Sydney was – by the Aviation journals the boys purchased in pre-war days. Sydney wrote in *A Lifetime of Design* for the Royal Aeronautical Society that "factors affecting the progress of aviation in the U.K. included the great contribution made by journals such as *Flight, The Aero* and *The Aeroplane*. He considered that they did an enormous amount to stimulate thought and arouse the enthusiasm of the younger generation. These journals – and those edited by F.J. – are now an important source of information about the past – they recorded what has become history, and told everyone what was happening in the rest of the world.

As news of research for this biography spread, I have received a number of communications regarding F.J.'s reputation and works. His reputation still lives, especially with senior citizens. Many wireless apprentices – as for the BBC – had recourse to F.J.'s books and journals for their "apprentice piece" tasks – one such remarked to me that in the 1960s there was nothing else of use on the bookshelves.

As an engineer, F.J. understood and catered for the needs of the community he served so well.

The following Appendix lists publications (excluding journals) of F.J. Camm and includes the one book published by Sydney Camm, *Aeroplane Construction* in 1919.

Appendix

Extracts from the British Museum Library Catalogue, Pages 30-31

The Books of Frederick James CAMM

(and Sir Sydney Camm)

CAMM (Frederick James) See also Waysider, pseud. [i.e. F. J. Camm.]

—— See Hunter (Norman) of Bromley. Norman Hunter's Successful Conjuring for Amateurs. Edited by F. J. Camm. [1951.] 8°.   7921. b. 12.

—— See Periodical Publications.—London.—*Practical Mechanics.* The First "Practical Mechanics" How-to-make-it Book. Edited by F. J. Camm, *etc.* 1961. 8°.   X. 441/347.

—— See Periodical Publications. London. *Practical Mechanics.* The "Practical Mechanics" How-to-make-it Book. Edited by F. J. Camm, *etc.* 1954. 8°.   7950. c. 7.

—— See Periodical Publications.—London.—*Practical Mechanics.* The Second "Practical Mechanics" How-to-make-it Book. Edited by F. J. Camm, *etc.* 1957. 8°.   8764. r. 9.

—— Accumulators. Charging, maintenance and care, *etc.* pp. 96. London, [1932.] 8°. [Newnes' Home Mechanic Books.]   07941. p. 51/6.

—— Amplifiers: design and construction. Edited by F. J. Camm, *etc.* pp. 280. George Newnes: London, 1957. 8°.   8761. eee. 40.

—— A Beginner's Guide to Radio, *etc.* pp. 160. George Newnes: London, 1955. 8°.   8762. de. 12.

—— A Beginner's Guide to Radio, *etc.* (Second edition.) pp. 160. George Newnes: London, 1956. 8°.   8762. e. 40.

—— A Beginner's Guide to Radio, *etc.* (Third edition.) pp. 160. George Newnes: London, 1957. 8°.   8762. f. 9.

—— A Beginner's Guide to Radio, *etc.* (Fourth edition.) pp. 160. George Newnes: London, 1959. 8°.   8762. p. 33.

—— A Beginner's Guide to Radio, *etc.* (Fifth edition.) pp. 160. George Newnes: London, 1960. 8°.   8778. s. 18.

CAMM (Frederick James)

—— A Beginner's Guide to Radio. An elementary course in 28 lessons. (Sixth edition.) [By F. J. Camm. With illustrations.] pp. 164. George Newnes: London, 1964. 8°.   X. 629/395
A later edition is entered under King (Gordon J.)

—— A Beginner's Guide to Television. An elementary course, *etc.* pp. 128. George Newnes: London, 1958. 8°.   8761. eee. 43.

—— A Beginner's Guide to Television, *etc.* (Second edition.) pp. 128. George Newnes: London, 1959. 8°.   8762. p. 35.
A later edition is entered under Beginner.

—— The Book of Motors, *etc.* [With plates.] pp. 256. Collins: London & Glasgow, [1932.] 8°.   08769. cc. 27.

—— Book of the B.S.A. . . . Sixth edition. pp. vii. 141. London, 1933. 8°. [*Pitman's Motor-Cyclists Library.*]   W.P. 8199/41.

—— Seventh edition. pp. vii. 149. London, 1935. 8°. [*Pitman's Motor-Cyclists Library.*]   W.P. 8199/46.

—— Seventh edition, reprinted. pp. vii. 155. London, 1935. 8°. [*Pitman's Motor-Cyclists Library.*]   W.P. 8199/53.

—— Eighth edition. pp. vii. 131. London, 1937. 8°. [*Pitman's Motor-Cyclists Library.*]   W.P. 8199/60.
Subsequent editions are entered under Haycraft (W. C.)

—— Book of the New Imperial, *etc.* pp. vii. 118. Sir I. Pitman & Sons: London, 1929. 8°. [*Motor-Cyclist's Library.*]   W.P. 8199/21.

—— Second edition. pp. vii. 128. Sir I. Pitman & Sons: London, 1932. 8°. [*Motor-Cyclists' Library.*]   W.P. 8199/35.

—— Third edition. pp. vii. 126. London, 1934. 8°. [*Pitman's Motor-Cyclist's Library.*]   W.P. 8199/43.

—— Fourth edition. pp. vii. 138. London, 1935. 8°. [*Pitman's Motor-Cyclist's Library.*]   W.P. 8199/55.
The fifth edition is entered under I., N.

—— Capstan and Turret Lathe Handbook, *etc.* pp. 350. George Newnes: London, 1957. 8°.   8772. aa. 60.

—— A Dictionary of Metals and their Alloys, their composition and characteristics, *etc.* pp. 244. George Newnes: London, 1940. 8°.   07107. f. 31.

—— Dictionary of Metals and Alloys . . . Third edition. pp. 176. George Newnes: London, 1944. 8°.   7111. a. 6.

—— Diesel Vehicles. Operation, maintenance and repair. Edited by F. J. Camm, *etc.* pp. 109. George Newnes: London, 1940. 8°.   08770. aa. 60.

—— Diesel Vehicles. Operation, maintenance and repair, *etc.* (Fourth edition.) pp. 107. George Newnes: London, [1946.] 8°.   8772. a. 55.

—— Diesel Vehicles, *etc.* (Sixth edition.) pp. 107. George Newnes: London, 1957. 8°.   8771. e. 24.
A later edition is entered under Fenton (A. E. N.)

—— The Elements of Mechanics and Mechanisms, *etc.* pp. 431. George Newnes: London, 1956. 8°.   8714. h. 4.

—— Every Cyclist's Handbook, *etc.* pp. 199. George Newnes: London, 1936. 8°.   08770. b. 18

—— Every Cyclist's Pocket Book. pp. viii. 399. George Newnes: London, [1950.] obl. 12°.   8767. e. 43

—— Every Cyclist's Pocket Book . . . Third edition. pp. viii. 395. George Newnes: London, 1953. obl. 12°.   8767. de. 44

CAMM (FREDERICK JAMES)

—— Everyman's Wireless Book. *See infra*: Newnes' Everyman's Wireless Book.

—— Fifty Tested Wireless Circuits. *See infra*: Twenty-Five Tested Wireless Circuits.

—— The Flying Reference Book. A guide to the history and development of all types of aircraft . . . Fully illustrated. pp. 207. *C. A. Pearson: London*, 1939. 8°.
08770. cc. 48.

—— The Flying Reference Book . . . 2nd edition. pp. 207. *C. A. Pearson: London*, 1940. 8°. 08771. aa. 10.

—— Gears and Gear-Cutting . . . Edited by F. J. Camm, etc. pp. 144. *George Newnes: London*, 1940. 8°.
08770. aa. 61.

—— The Home Electrician. pp. 206. *C. Arthur Pearson: London*, 1956. 8°. 8762. p. 8.

—— The Home Electrician. (Second edition.) pp. 219. *C. Arthur Pearson: London*, 1959. 8°. 7837. b. 15.

—— The Home Electrician. (Third edition.) [With illustrations.] pp. 226. *C. Arthur Pearson: London*, 1962. 8°.
X. 629/216.

—— The Home Electrician. Fourth edition. [By F. J. Camm. With illustrations.] pp. 228. *C. Arthur Pearson: London*, 1964. 8°. X. 449/559.

—— The Home Electrician. A practical handbook on the installation of electrical apparatus, etc. pp. 96. *London*, [1938.] 8°. [*Newnes' Home Mechanic Books.*]
07941.p.51/14.

—— The Home Mechanic Encyclopaedia, etc. pp. 392. *George Newnes: London*, [1935.] 8°. 07945. k. 57.

—— Lathework for Amateurs, etc. pp. 96. *London*, 1935. 8°. [*Newnes' Home Mechanic Books.*]
07941.p.51/12.

—— Make your own Wireless Set. pp. 80. *George Newnes: London*, [1932.] 8°. 08755. bb. 49.

—— Marvels of Modern Science. Very fully illustrated. pp. 192. *George Newnes: London*, 1935. 4°.
8710. h. 23.

—— (Revised edition.) pp. 192. *George Newnes: London*, 1938. 4°. 08712. dd. 2.

—— Mastering Morse, etc. pp. 31. *George Newnes: London*, [1941.] 8°. 8760. aa. 14.

—— Mathematical Tables and Formulæ for Engineers, etc. *George Newnes: London*, 1943. obl. 24°. 08548. b. 44.

—— Mathematical Tables and Formulae for Engineers & Technical Students. (Fourth edition.) pp. 156. *George Newnes: London*, 1949. obl. 12°. 08548. b. 55.

—— Mathematical Tables and Formulæ for Engineers & Technical Students . . . Fifth edition. pp. 144. *George Newnes: London*, 1954. obl. 12°. 08548. ff. 100.

—— Mathematical Tables and Formulae for Engineers & Technical Students. (Sixth edition.) pp. 145. *George Newnes: London*, 1957. 12°. 08548. pp. 1.

—— Mechanical Drawing. With 256 illustrations. [By F. J. Camm and others.] pp. 263. *London*, [1921.] 8°. [*Cassell's Workshop Series.*] W.P. 5728/2.

—— Model Aeroplane Handbook, etc. pp. viii. 320. *George Newnes: London*, 1949. 8°. 7949. aa. 8.

—— Model Aeroplanes. The building of model monoplanes, biplanes, etc., together with a chapter on building a model airship, etc. pp. 156. *Cassell & Co.: London*, [1920.] 8°. [" Work " Handbooks.] D-07943. cc. 10/41.

CAMM (FREDERICK JAMES)

—— Model Aeroplanes and Airships, etc. pp. 96. *London*, [1931.] 8°. [*Newnes' Home Mechanics Series.*]
07941.p.51/1

—— The Model Aircraft Book . . . With 231 illustration pp. 143. *Newnes: London*, [1936.] 4°. D-07942. f. 1

—— (Revised edition.) pp. 147. *George Newnes: London*, 1938. 4°. D - 7944. v. 2

—— Model Boat Building, etc. pp. 144. *George Newnes: London*, 1940. 8°. 8804. df. 9

—— Model Engineering Practice. pp. 235. *George Newnes: London*, 1957. 8°. 8772. aa. 58

—— More Miles per Gallon. How to reduce your petrol consumption, etc. pp. 96. *George Newnes: London*, [1939.] 8°. 08770. aaa. 7

—— More Miles per Gallon. How to reduce your petrol consumption. pp. 96. *George Newnes: London*, 1957. 8°.
8771. de. 17

—— Motor Car Principles and Practice, etc. pp. 184. *George Newnes: London*, 1940. 8°. 08770. aa. 51

—— Motor Car Principles and Practice, etc. (Seventh edition.) pp. 188. *George Newnes: London*, 1956. 8°.
08774. c. 60

—— Motor Car Upkeep and Overhaul, etc. pp. 96. *London*, [1932.] 8°. [*Newnes' Home Mechanic Books.*]
07841.p.51/10

—— Newnes Engineer's Manual . . . Second edition. pp. 256. *George Newnes: London*, 1940. 8°. 08771. a. 4

—— Newnes Engineer's Manual, etc. (Fifth edition, revised and enlarged.) pp. ix. 334. *George Newnes: London*, 1958. 8°. 08770. ee. 7

—— [A reissue.] Newnes Engineer's Manual, etc. [1965.] 8° *See* NEWNES (George) LTD. X. 629/738

—— Newnes Engineer's Pocket Book of Tables, Formulæ and Memoranda. pp. 603. *George Newnes: London*, [1942.] obl. 12°. 8767. a. 94

—— Newnes Engineer's Pocket Book of Tables, Formula [sic] and Memoranda. (Third edition.) pp. 619. *George Newnes: London*, 1949. obl. 12°. 8771. a. 41

—— Newnes Engineer's Pocket Book of Tables, Formula [sic] and Memoranda. (Fourth edition.) pp. 626. *George Newnes: London*, 1958. obl. 12°. 08765. a. 12.

—— Newnes Engineer's Pocket Book of Tables, Formula [sic] and Memoranda. (Fifth edition.) pp. 620. *George Newnes: London*, 1964. obl. 8°. X. 629/404.
A later edition is entered under NAYLOR (Gerald).

—— Newnes Engineer's Reference Book. Edited by F. J. Camm. pp. 1326. *George Newnes: London*, 1946. 8°.
8775. aaaa. 23

—— Newne's Engineer's Reference Book. Edited by F. J. Camm . . . Second edition. pp. 1378. *George Newnes: London*, 1947. 8°. 08771. a. 42

—— Newnes Engineer's Reference Book. (Third edition.) pp. 1608. *George Newnes: London*, 1949. 8°.
8771.a.30.

—— [Another copy.] Newnes Engineer's Reference Book, etc. *London*, 1949. 8°. 08769. a. 121.

—— Newnes Engineer's Reference Book. Edited by F. J. Camm. (Fourth edition.) pp. 1727. *George Newnes: London*, 1951. 8°. 8771.de.18.

CAMM (FREDERICK JAMES)

—— Newnes Engineer's Reference Book. Edited by F. J. Camm. (Fifth edition.) pp. 1909. *George Newnes: London,* 1952. 8°.   **8774. a. 3.**

—— Newnes Engineer's Reference Book. Edited by F. J. Camm. (Sixth edition.) pp. 1970. *George Newnes: London,* 1954. 8°.   **8774. a. 29.**

—— Newnes Engineer's Reference Book. Edited by F. J. Camm. (Seventh edition.) pp. 2028. *George Newnes: London,* 1956. 8°.   **X. 629/2, 35.**

—— [Another copy.] Newnes Engineer's Reference Book, *etc.* (Seventh edition.) *London,* 1956. 8°.   **8772. aa. 54.**

—— Newnes Engineer's Reference Book. Edited by F. J. Camm. (Eighth edition.) pp. 2034. *George Newnes: London,* 1958. 8°.   **08763. aa. 3.**

—— Newnes Engineer's Reference Book. Edited by F. J. Camm. (Ninth edition.) Revised by A. T. Collins pp. 2067. *George Newnes: London,* 1960. 8°.   **8779. g. 45.**

—— [Another copy.] Newnes Engineer's Reference Book, *etc. London,* 1960. 8°.   **8780. cc. 8.**

—— Newnes Engineer's Reference Book. Revised by A. T. Collins. (Tenth edition [of the work edited by F. J. Camm].) pp. 2066. *George Newnes: London,* 1965. 8°.   **X. 629/959.**

—— Everyman's Wireless Book, *etc.* pp. 287. *George Newnes: London,* 1934. 8°.   **8759. ccc. 39.**

—— Everyman's Wireless Book, *etc.* (Revised edition [of the author's " Newnes' Everyman's Wireless Book "].) pp. 287. *George Newnes: London,* 1939. 8°.   **08756. b. 40.**

—— Everyman's Wireless Book, *etc.* (Eleventh edition.) pp. 295. *George Newnes: London,* 1952. 8°.   **08755. aa. 69.**

—— Everyman's Wireless Book, *etc.* (Twelfth edition.) pp. 296. *George Newnes: London,* 1956. 8°.   **8762. e. 39.**

—— Everyman's Wireless Book, *etc.* (Thirteenth edition.) pp. 296. *George Newnes: London,* 1959. 8°.   **8762. h. 65.**

—— Newnes Metric and Decimal Tables. pp. 149. *George Newnes: London,* 1947. obl. 12°.   **08548. b. 47.**

—— Newnes Metric and Decimal Tables . . . 2nd edition. pp. 149. *George Newnes: London,* 1954. obl. 12°.   **08548. bb. 12.**

—— Newnes Metric and Decimal Tables. 3rd edition. pp. 149. *George Newnes: London,* 1963. obl. 12°.   **8508. m. 28.**

—— Newnes Plastics Manual. By F. J. Camm, H. W. Gilbert-Rolfe and D. C. Nicholas. pp. viii. 272. *George Newnes: London,* 1945. 8°.   **7946. c. 37.**

—— Newnes Plastics Manual. By F. J. Camm, H. W. Gilbert-Rolfe and D. C. Nicholas. (Second edition.) pp. viii. 276. *George Newnes: London,* 1947. 8°.   **7940. ff. 7.**

—— Newnes Radio Valve Data Pocket Book. pp. 108. *George Newnes: London,* 1945. obl. 12°.   **8758. a. 48.**

—— Newnes Short-Wave Manual, *etc.* pp. 211. *George Newnes: London,* 1940. 8°.   **08757. aa. 13.**

—— Newnes Short-Wave Manual. (Seventh edition.) pp. 200. *George Newnes: London,* 1949. 8°.   **8753. a. 17.**

CAMM (FREDERICK JAMES)

—— Newnes' Slide Rule Manual. pp. 112. *George Newnes: London,* 1944. 8°.   **08534. de. 64.**

—— Newnes' Slide Rule Manual. (Fifth edition.) pp. 112. *George Newnes: London,* 1953. 8°.   **8536. a. 22.**

—— Newnes' Slide Rule Manual. (Sixth edition.) pp. 112. *George Newnes: London,* 1957. 8°.   **8535. b. 56.**

—— Newnes' Slide Rule Manual. (Seventh edition.) pp. 112. *George Newnes: London,* 1963. 8°.   **8509. bb. 25.**

—— Newnes Television and Short-Wave Handbook. With 230 illustrations. pp. 255. *George Newnes: London,* 1934. 8°.   **08756. bb. 6.**

—— Television and Short-Wave Handbook . . . Fourth edition. pp. 271. *George Newnes: London,* 1939. 8°.   **08757. b. 5.**

—— Newnes Television Manual . . . Fifth edition [of " Television and Short-Wave Handbook "]. pp. 224. *George Newnes: London,* 1942. 8°.   **8760. aa. 33.**

—— Newnes Television Manual, *etc.* (Seventh edition.) pp. 224. *George Newnes: London,* 1948. 8°.   **8758. bbb. 39.**

—— Power-Driven Model Aircraft, *etc.* pp. 96. *London,* [1934.] 8°. [*Newnes' Home Mechanic Books.* no. 15.]   **07941. p. 51/9.**

—— Practical Mechanics Handbook. Facts, figures, tables, and formulæ for the mechanic, *etc.* pp. 400. *George Newnes: London,* 1938. 8°.   **8771. aa. 7.**

—— Practical Mechanics Handbook, *etc.* (Seventh—revised —edition.) pp. 400. *George Newnes: London,* 1949. 8°.   **8771. a. 37.**

—— Practical Mechanics Handbook, *etc.* (Eighth edition.) pp. 400. *George Newnes: London,* 1956. 8°.   **08774. g. 52.**

—— The Practical Motorist's Encyclopædia. Principles, upkeep and repair of every part of the car. With 442 illustrations. pp. vii. 392. [1935.] 8°. *See* ENCYCLOPAEDIAS.   **08770. aaa. 2.**

—— (New edition.) pp. 397. 1939. 8°. *See* ENCYCLOPAEDIAS.   **08770. cc. 47.**

—— The Practical Motorist's Encyclopædia, *etc.* (Seventh edition.) pp. 377. 1948. 8°. *See* ENCYCLOPÆDIAS.   **8772. aa. 50.**

—— The Practical Motorist's Encyclopædia, *etc.* (Eighth edition, revised.) pp. 378. *George Newnes: London,* 1952. 8°.   **08766. aaa. 57.**

—— The Practical Motorist's Encyclopædia, *etc.* (Ninth edition.) pp. 477. *George Newnes: London,* 1958. 8°.   **08765. aa. 29.**

—— Practical Television Circuits. With additional chapter on test apparatus and auxiliary equipment, *etc.* pp. 288. *George Newnes: London,* 1954. 8°.   **8761. ccc. 7.**

—— Practical Wireless Circuits. *See infra:* Twenty-Five Tested Wireless Circuits.

—— The Practical Wireless Encyclopædia, *etc. See infra:* Wireless Constructor's Encyclopædia.

—— Practical Wireless Service Manual, *etc.* pp. 295. *George Newnes: London,* 1938. 8°.   **08757. b. 4.**

—— Practical Wireless Service Manual . . . 2nd edition, *etc.* pp. 296. *George Newnes: London,* 1940. 8°.   **2244. d. 26.**

—— Practical Wireless Service Manual . . . Edited by F. J. Camm, *etc.* (Ninth edition.) pp. 296. *George Newnes: London,* 1950. 8°.   **08757. bb. 39.**

—— Practical Wireless Service Manual, *etc.* (Tenth edition.) pp. 290. *George Newnes: London,* 1955. 8°.   **8761. de. 47.**

CAMM (FREDERICK JAMES)
— Practical Wireless Service Manual, *etc.* (Eleventh edition. Revised by A. T. Collins.) pp. 302. *George Newnes: London*, 1960. 8°. *A later edition is entered under Practical Publications — London — Practical Wireless.* 8762. h. 83.

— Radio-controlled Models. pp. 184. *C. Arthur Pearson: London*, [1958.] 8°. 8762. p. 25.

— Radio-Controlled Models. (Second edition.) [Revised and with a new chapter on "Model-Control Aerial Efficiency" by A. T. Collins.] pp. 192. *C. Arthur Pearson: London*, 1963. 8°. 8761. a. 94.

— Radio Engineer's Pocket Book. pp. 147. *George Newnes: London*, 1940. 12°. 8758. a. 45.

— Radio Engineer's Pocket Book . . . Ninth edition. pp. 207. *George Newnes: London*, 1949. 12°. 8758. a. 26.

— Radio Engineer's Pocket Book . . . Tenth edition. pp. 181. *George Newnes: London*, 1953. 12°. 8755. a. 66.

— Radio Engineer's Pocket Book . . . Eleventh edition. pp. 177. *George Newnes: London*, 1955. 12°. 8755. a. 67.

— Radio Engineer's Pocket Book . . . Twelfth edition. pp. 177. *George Newnes: London*, 1958. obl. 12°. 8762. f. 15.
A later edition is entered under COLLINS (Albert T.)

— Radio Training Manual. For the services and the trade. Edited by F. J. Camm, *etc.* pp. 160. *George Newnes: London*, [1940.] 8°. 08757. b. 15.

— Radio Valve Data Pocket Book . . . Second edition. pp. 198. *George Newnes: London*, 1947. obl. 12°. 8761. a. 6.

— A Refresher Course in Mathematics, *etc.* pp. 240. *George Newnes: London*, 1943. 8°. 08534. g. 50.

— A Refresher Course in Mathematics, *etc.* (Fifth edition.) pp. 240. *George Newnes: London*, 1956. 8°. 8508. eee. 27.

— Screw Cutting. With . . . illustrations. pp. vi. 263. *London*, [1920.] 8°. [*Cassell's Workshop Series.*] W.P. 5728/3.

— Screw Thread Tables. pp. 214. *George Newnes: London*, 1943. obl. 12°. 08548. b. 46.

— Screw Thread Tables . . . Third edition. pp. 224. *George Newnes: London*, 1955. 12°. 8548. a. 88.

— Screw Thread Tables. Fourth edition. pp. 227. *George Newnes: London*, 1964. obl. 8°. X. 629/405.

— Sixty Tested Wireless Circuits. *See infra*: Twenty-Five Tested Wireless Circuits.

— The Superhet Manual . . . Edited by F. J. Camm, *etc.* pp. 135. *George Newnes: London*, 1940. 8°. 08757. a. 27.

— The Superhet Manual, *etc.* (Fifth edition.) pp. 143. *George Newnes: London*, 1954. 8°. 8761. bb. 47.

— Television and Short-Wave Handbook. *See supra*: Newnes Television and Short-Wave Handbook.

— Television Principles and Practice. [With illustrations.] pp. 215. *George Newnes: London*, 1952. 8°. 8761. de. 35.

— Television Principles and Practice. (Second edition.) pp. 215. *George Newnes: London*, 1955. 8°. 8762. aa. 42.

— Twenty-five Tested Wireless Circuits . . . Edited by F. J. Camm, *etc.* pp. 96. *London*, [1931.] 8°. [*Newnes' Home Mechanic Books.*] 07941. p. 51/4.

CAMM (FREDERICK JAMES)
— Fifty Tested Wireless Circuits . . . Edited by F. J. Camm, *etc.* [A revised edition of "Twenty-Five Tested Wireless Circuits."] pp. 144. *George Newnes: London*, [1933.] 8°. 08756. aa. 20.

— Sixty Tested Wireless Circuits, *etc.* [Revised edition of "Fifty Tested Wireless Circuits."] pp. 168. *George Newnes: London*, [1938.] 8°. 8760. aa. 10.

— Practical Wireless Circuits . . . Formerly "Sixty Tested Wireless Circuits" . . . Tenth edition. pp. 168. *George Newnes: London*, 1941. 8°. 8760. aa. 9.

— Practical Wireless Circuits, *etc.* (Fifteenth edition.) pp. 174. *George Newnes: London*, 1949. 8°. 8761. bb. 6.

— Practical Wireless Circuits, *etc.* (Sixteenth edition.) pp. 222. *George Newnes: London*, 1954. 8°. 8761. eee. 10.

— Practical Wireless Circuits, *etc.* (Seventeenth edition.) pp. 294. *George Newnes: London*, 1957. 8°. 8761. de. 74.

— Watches: adjustment & repair, *etc.* pp. 166. *George Newnes: London*, 1940. 8°. 07941. pp. 43.

— Wire and Wire Gauges, with special section on wire ropes. pp. 139. *George Newnes: London*, 1941. 12°. 08548. b. 38.

— Wireless Coils, Chokes and Transformers, and how to make them . . . Edited by F. J. Camm. pp. 176. *George Newnes: London*, [1937.] 8°. 08756. a. 82.

— The Wireless Constructor's Encyclopædia, *etc.* pp. vii. 392. *George Newnes: London*, [1933.] 8°. 08756. bb. 2.

— Second edition. pp. vii. 392. *George Newnes: London*, [1933.] 8°. 08756. bb. 1.

— The Practical Wireless Encyclopædia . . . Seventh edition [of the "Wireless Constructor's Encyclopædia"], fully revised, *etc.* pp. viii. 394. *George Newnes: London*, 1939. 8°. 2244. d. 18.

— The Practical Wireless Encyclopædia . . . Eighth edition. pp. viii. 394. *George Newnes: London*, 1941. 8°. 8760. aa. 5.

— Practical Wireless Encylopaedia, *etc.* (Twelfth edition.) pp. xii. 372. *George Newnes: London*, 1951. 8°. 8753. eee. 71.

— Practical Wireless Encyclopaedia, *etc.* (Thirteenth edition.) pp. xii. 370. *George Newnes: London*, 1954. 8°. 8755. de. 34.

— Wireless Transmission for Amateurs, *etc.* pp. 143. *George Newnes: London*, 1938. 8°. 8759. de. 37.

— Working Models and how to make them. pp. 160. *George Newnes: London*, [1934.] 4°. D-7943. ppp. 18.

— Workshop Arithmetic, *etc.* pp. 152. *Cassell & Co.: London*, [1920.] 8°. ["*Work*" *Handbooks.*] D-07943. cc. 10/23.

— Workshop Arithmetic. With special chapters on using and reading the micrometer, vernier and slide-rule, *etc.* [For the most part by F. J. Camm.] pp. 152. *Cassell & Co.: London*, [1920.] 8°. [*Cassell's "Work" Handbooks.*] 7949. k. 1/25.

— Workshop Calculations, Tables and Formulae, *etc.* pp. 144. *George Newnes: London*, [1938.] 8°. 08548. aa. 26.

— Workshop Calculations, Tables and Formulæ, *etc.* (Tenth edition.) pp. 179. *George Newnes: London*, 1952. 8°. 08548. aaa. 60.

CAMM (Sir SYDNEY)
— Aeroplane Construction, *etc.* pp. viii. 138. *C. Lockwood & Son: London*, 1919. 8°. 08768. b. 22.